THIS HOW TO DRAW A UNICORN BOOK

BELONGS TO:

____

DEDICATION

This How to draw a Unicorn notebook is dedicated to all the Unicorn Lovers out there who are full of artsy ideas and want to share their inspirations with the world and document their findings in the process.

You are my inspiration for producing books and I'm honored to be a part of keeping all of your unicorn drawings organized all in one easy to find spot.

How to use this book:

The purpose of this book is to keep all of your unicorn drawings all in one place. It will help keep you organized.

Learning to draw is with the grid copy method. It's a wonderful way to work on your unicorn observations and proportion skills while drawing. Comes with over 30 magical illustrations!

This unicorn drawing sketchbook grid copy method will allow you to accurately document every detail about learning to draw unicorns. It's a great way to chart your course through learning how to draw different unicorns.

Here are examples of the prompts for you to fill in and write about your experience in this book:

1. Unicorn Drawing - For learning to draw different unicorns.

2. Your Turn - All your grid happy drawings. Use this space to practice drawing out unicorns.

Enjoy!

A B C D E F
1
2
3
4
5
6
7
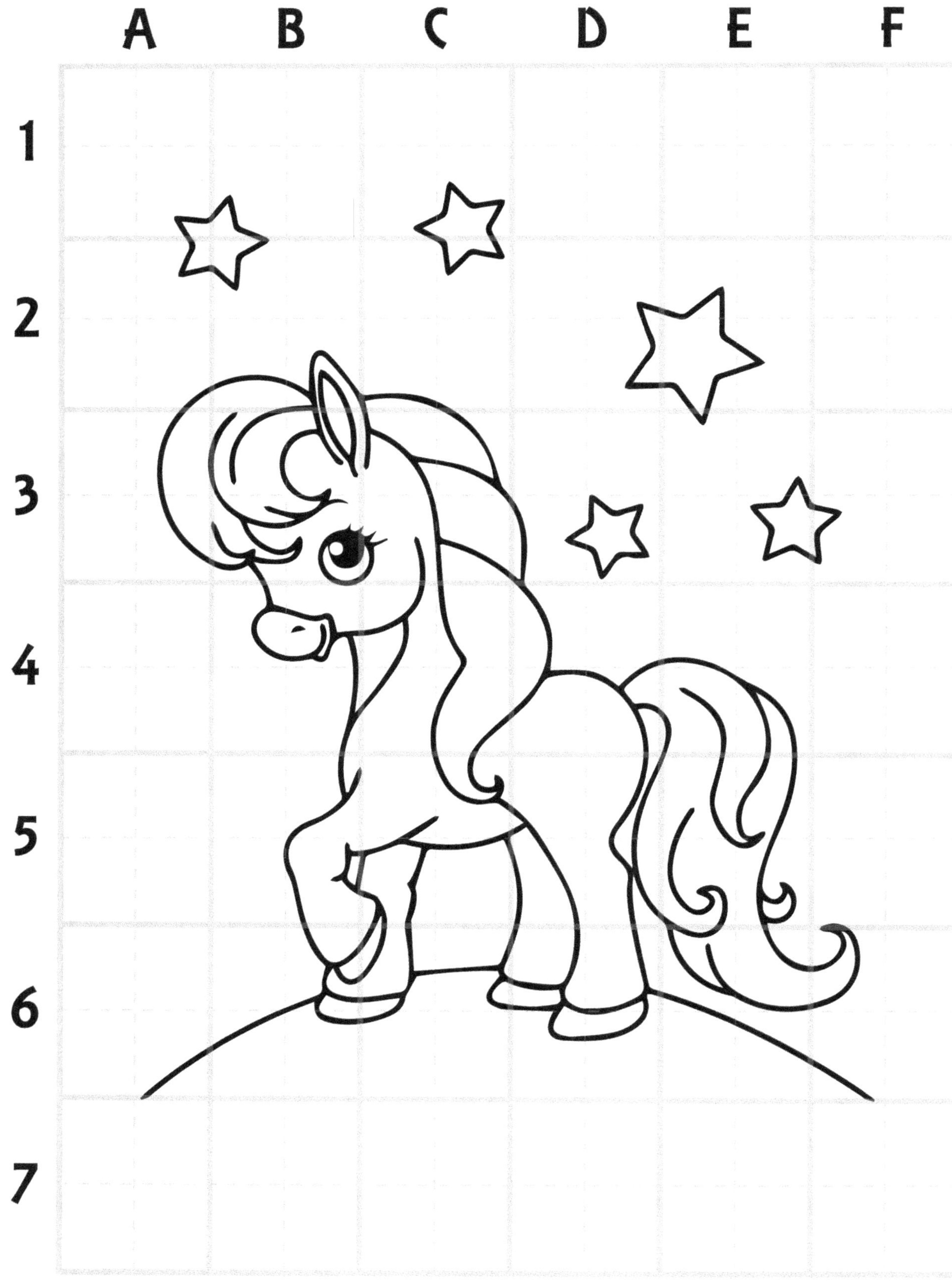

YOUR TURN!

	A	B	C	D	E	F
1						
2						
3						
4						
5						
6						
7						

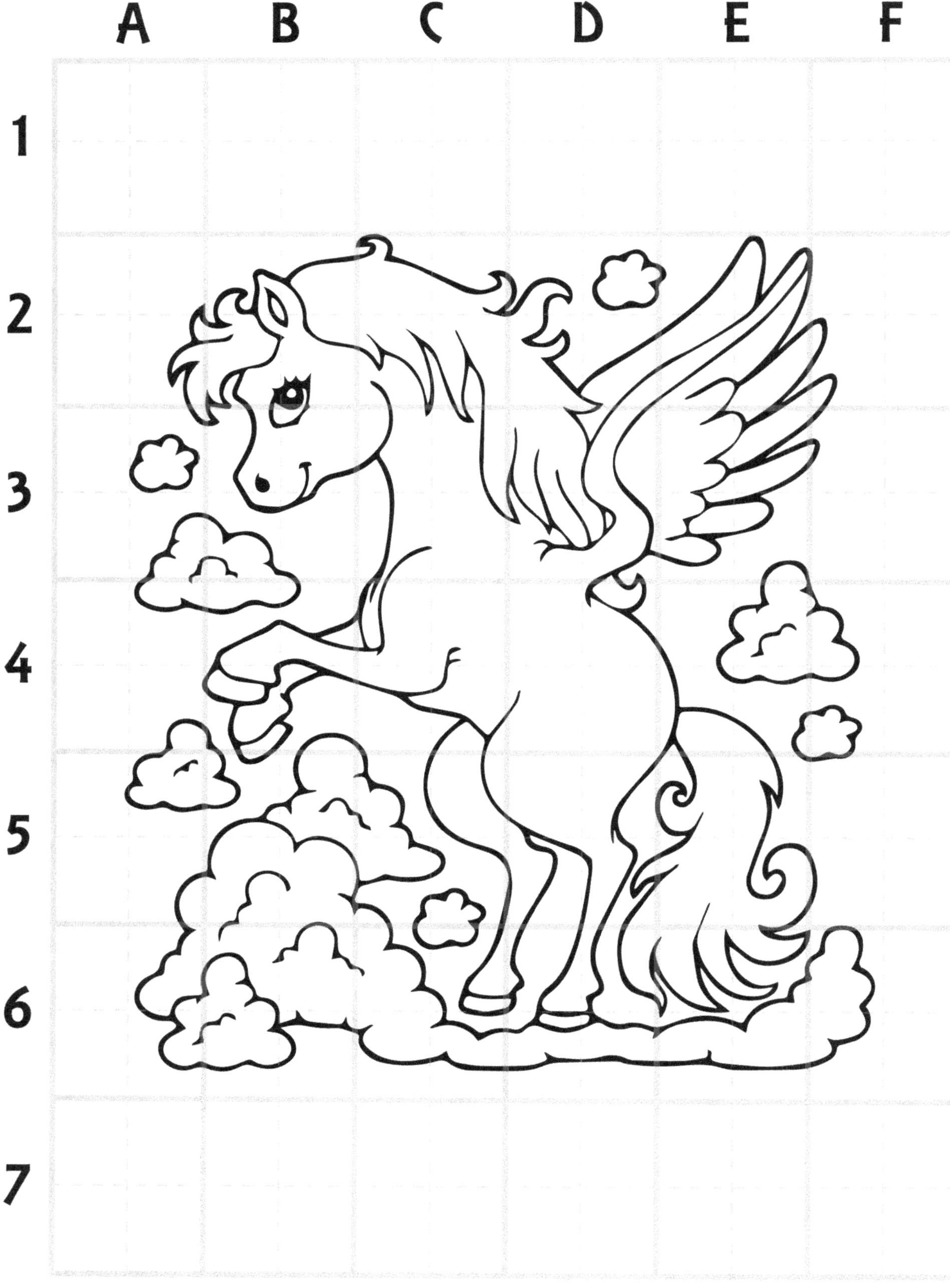

YOUR TURN!

	A	B	C	D	E	F
1						
2						
3						
4						
5						
6						
7						

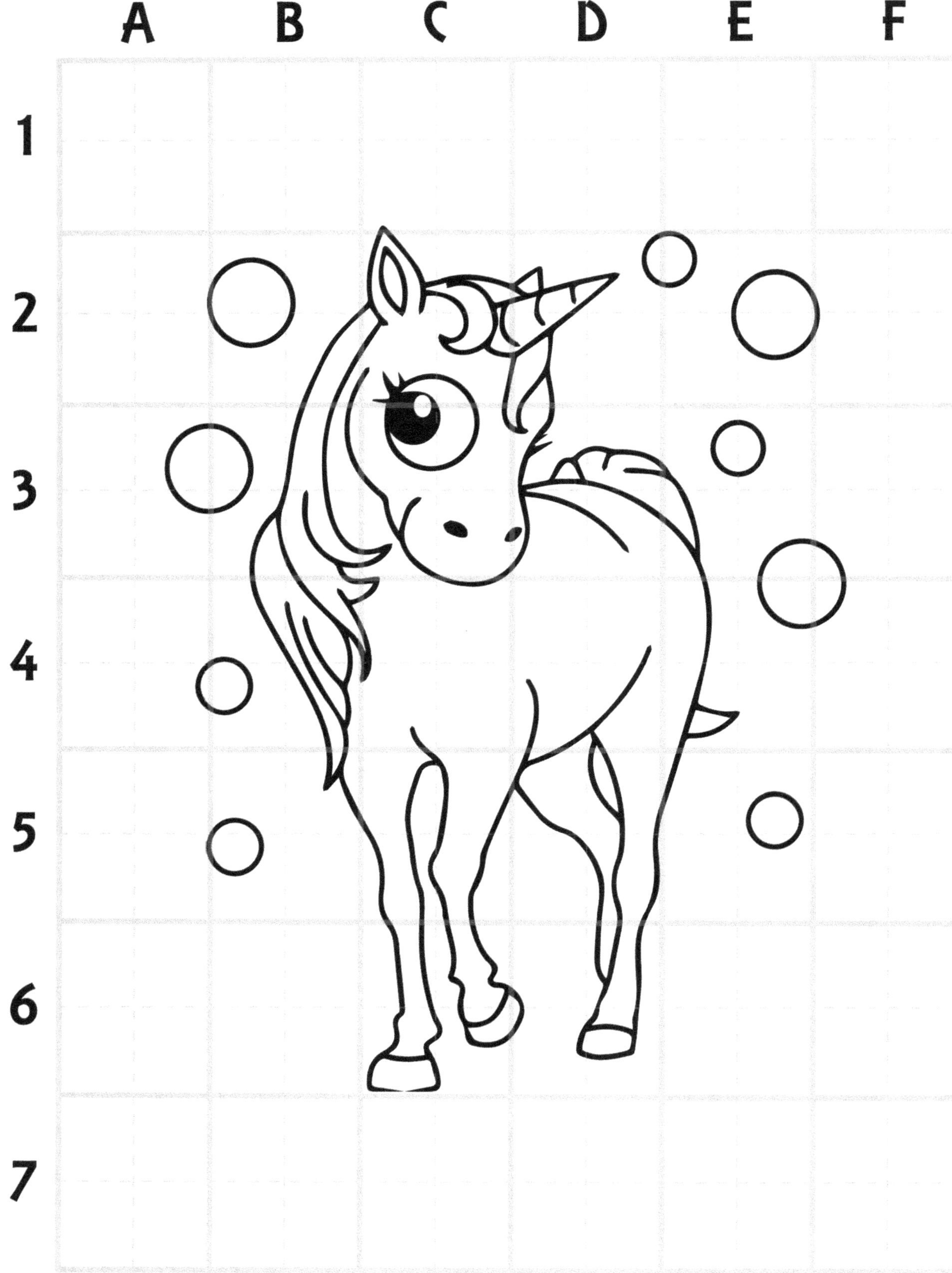

A B C D E F
1
2
3
4
5
6
7

YOUR TURN!

	A	B	C	D	E	F
1						
2						
3						
4						
5						
6						
7						

A B C D E F
1
2
3
4
5
6
7

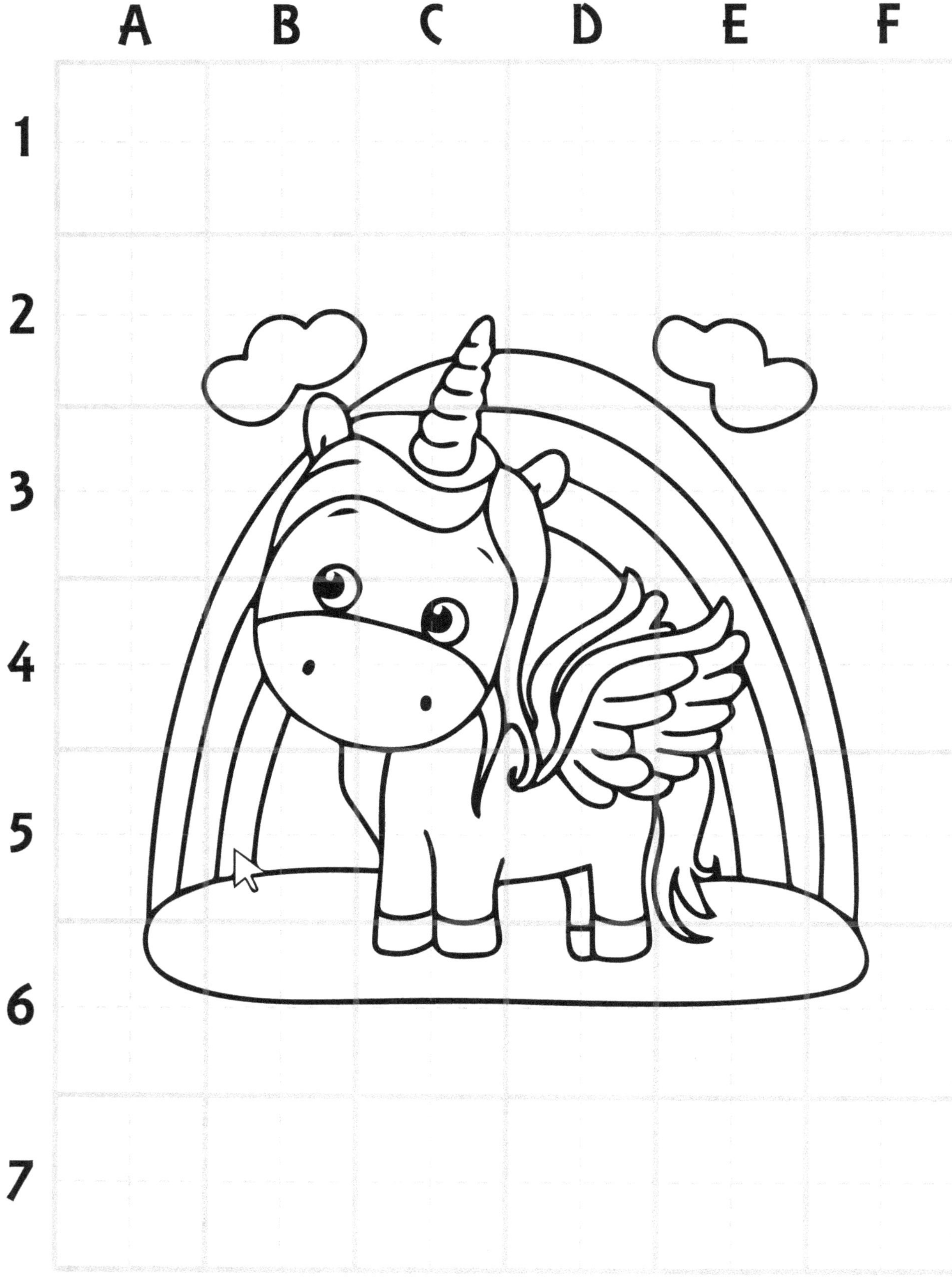

YOUR TURN!

	A	B	C	D	E	F
1						
2						
3						
4						
5						
6						
7						

A B C D E F

1 2 3 4 5 6 7

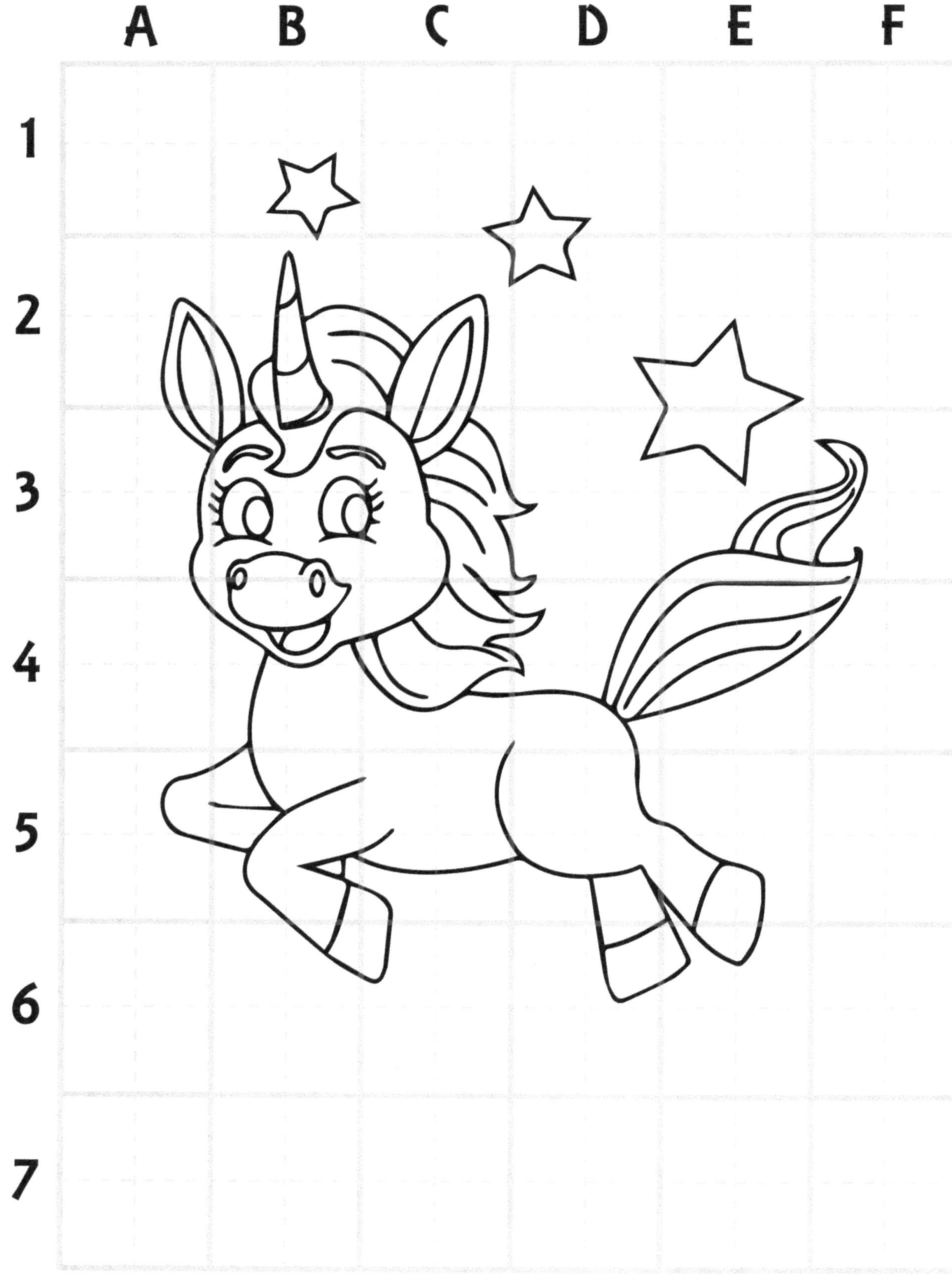

YOUR TURN!

	A	B	C	D	E	F
1						
2						
3						
4						
5						
6						
7						

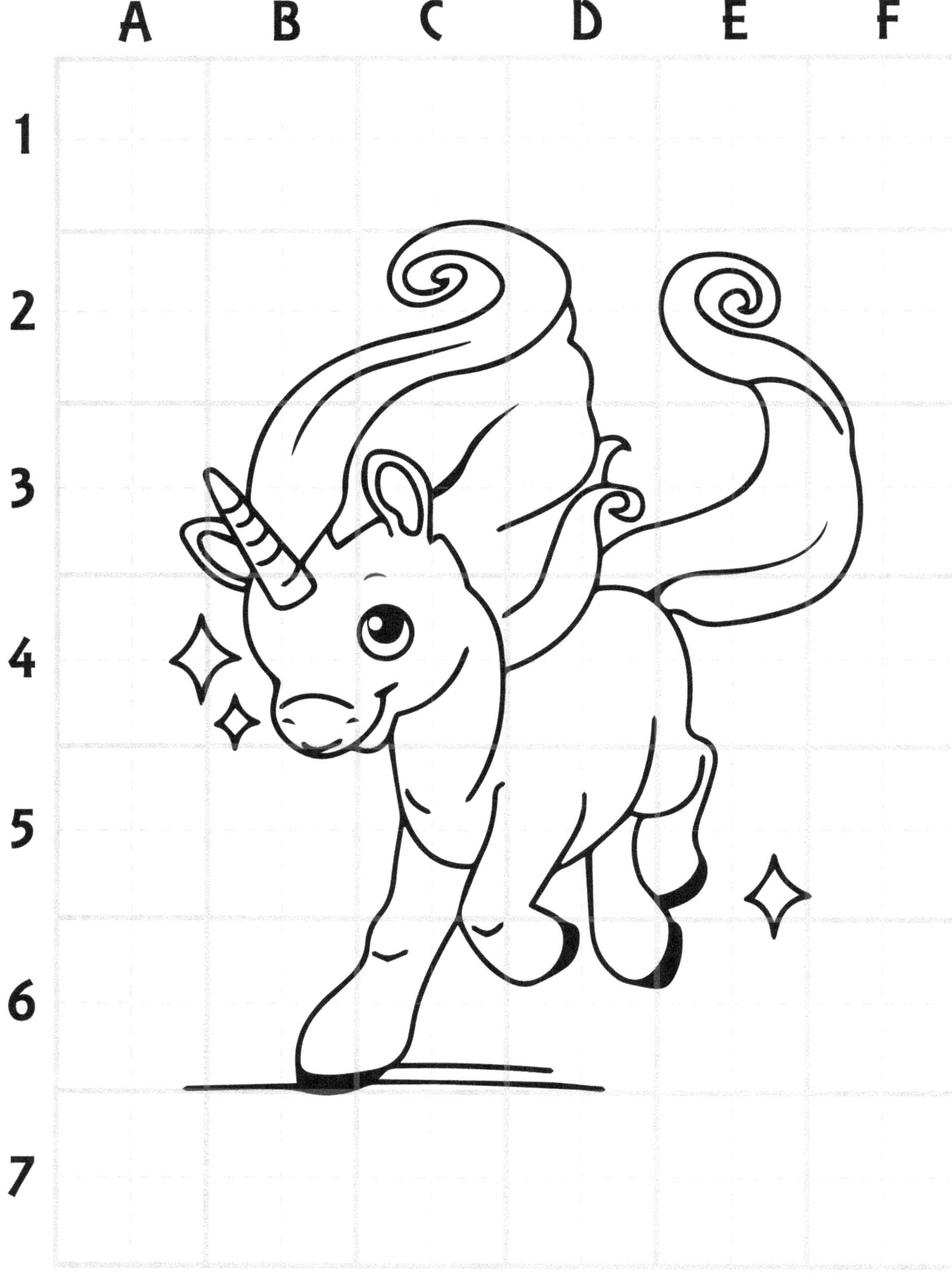
A B C D E F
1
2
3
4
5
6
7

YOUR TURN!

	A	B	C	D	E	F
1						
2						
3						
4						
5						
6						
7						

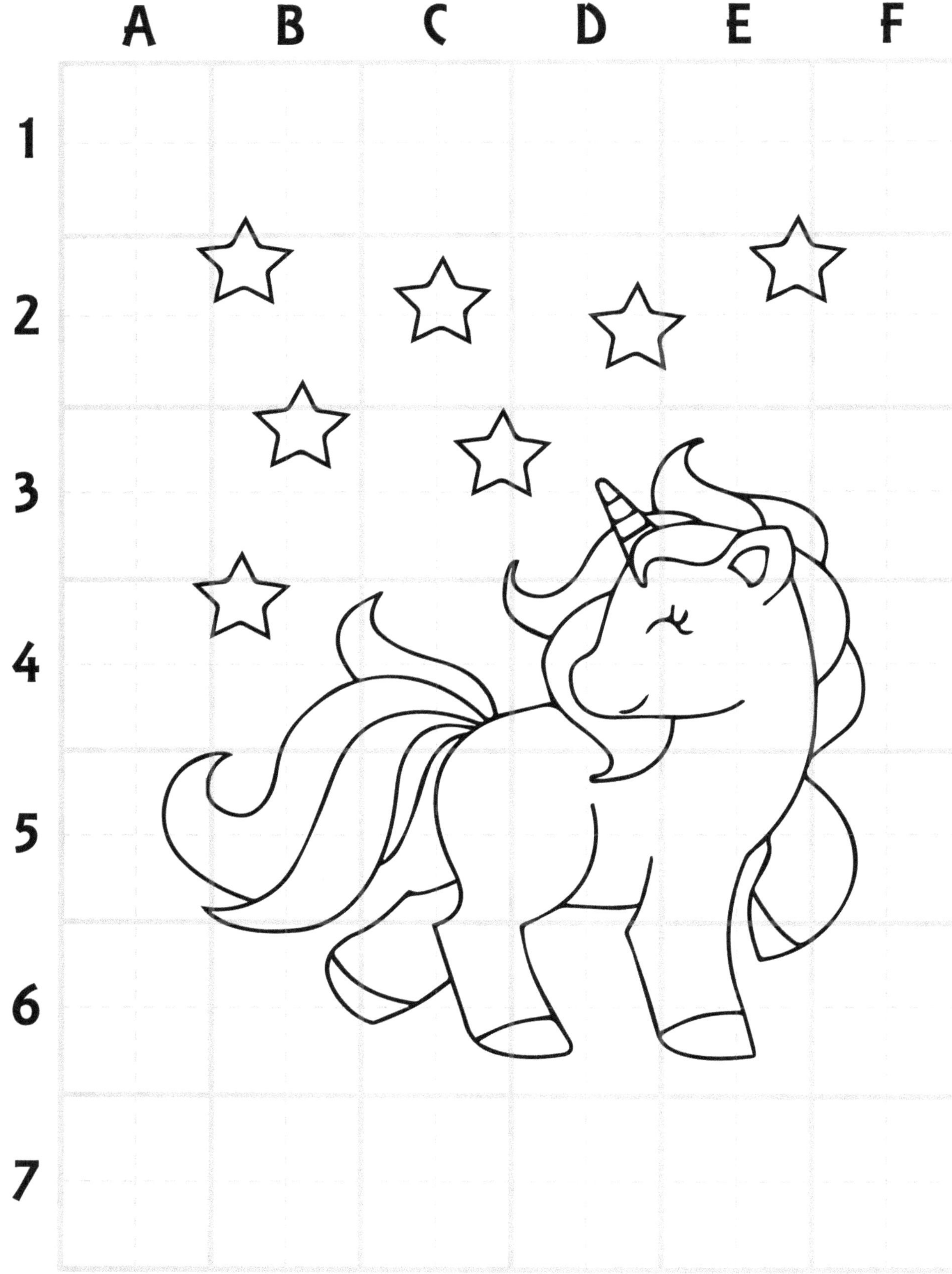

YOUR TURN!

	A	B	C	D	E	F
1						
2						
3						
4						
5						
6						
7						

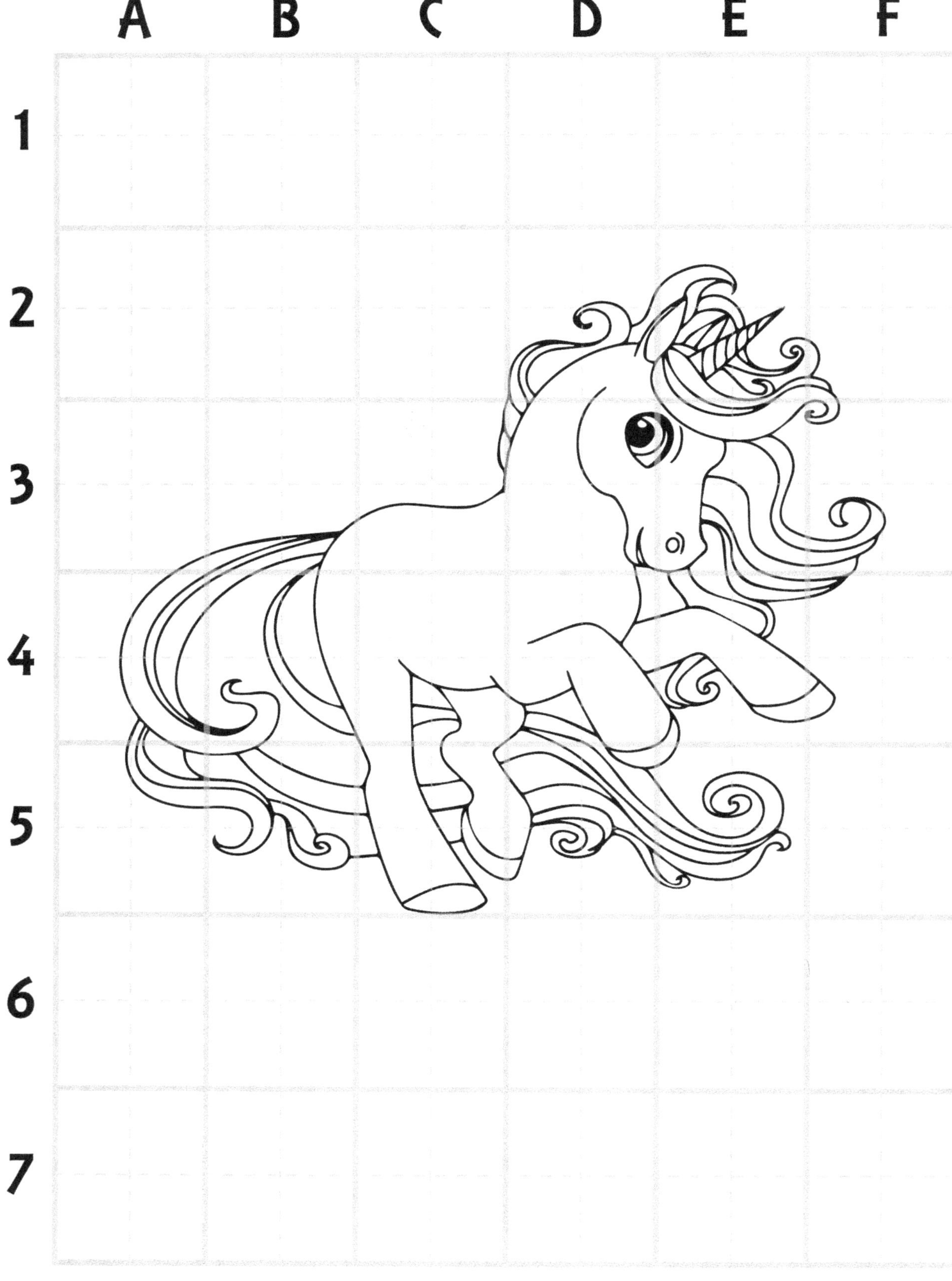

YOUR TURN!

	A	B	C	D	E	F
1						
2						
3						
4						
5						
6						
7						

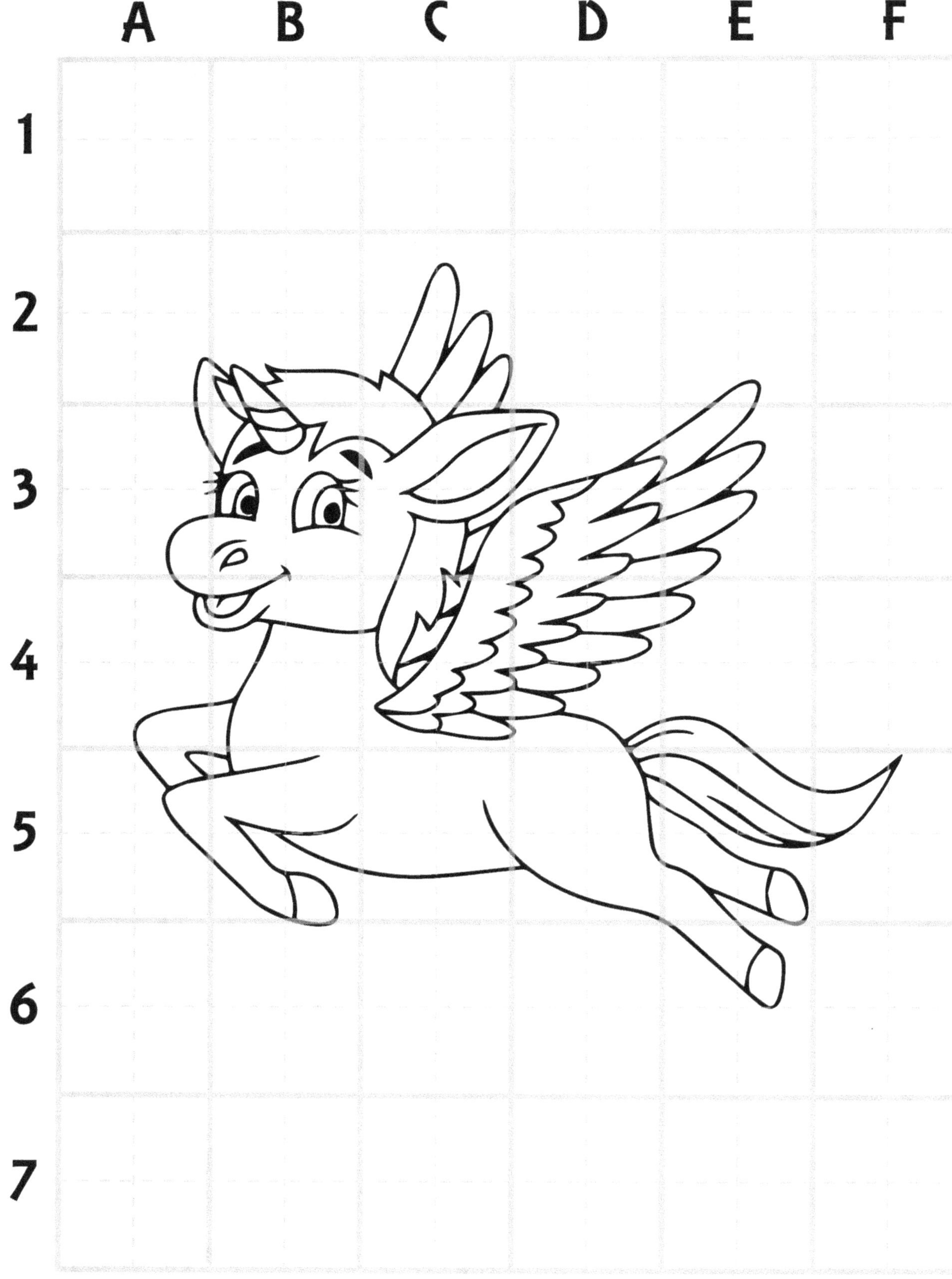

YOUR TURN!

	A	B	C	D	E	F
1						
2						
3						
4						
5						
6						
7						

	A	B	C	D	E	F

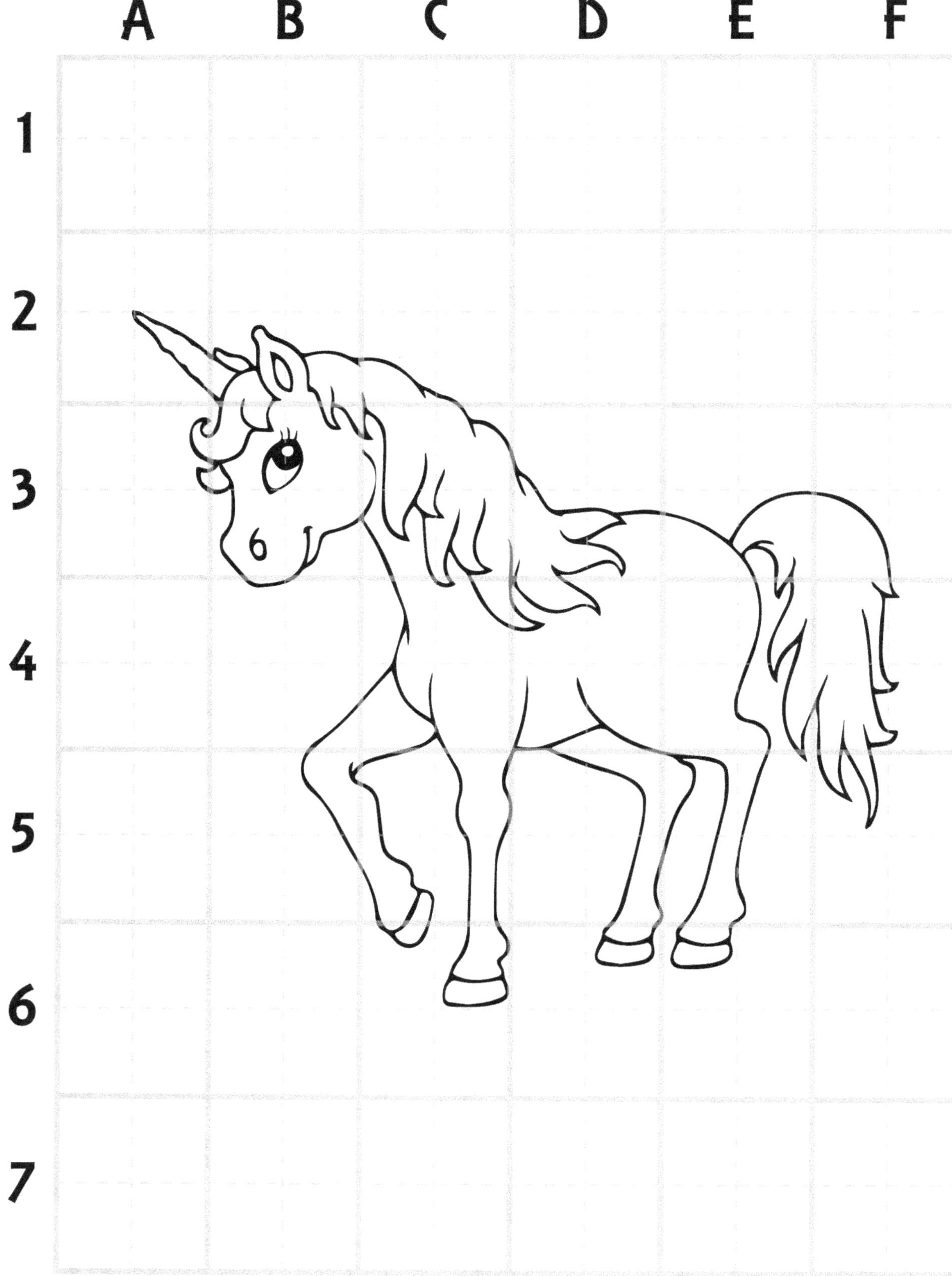

YOUR TURN!

	A	B	C	D	E	F
1						
2						
3						
4						
5						
6						
7						

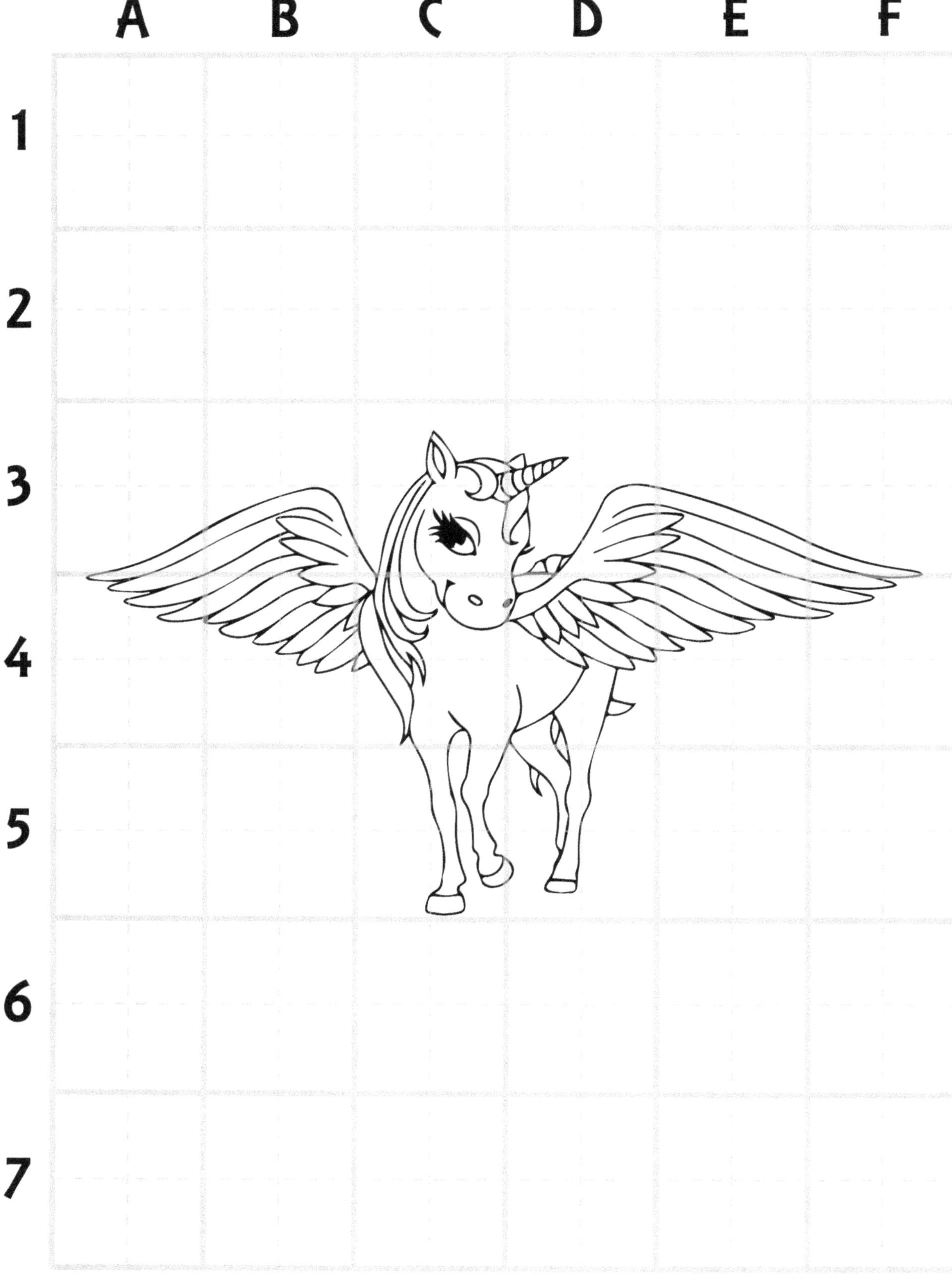

YOUR TURN!

	A	B	C	D	E	F
1						
2						
3						
4						
5						
6						
7						

A B C D E F
1
2
3
4
5
6
7

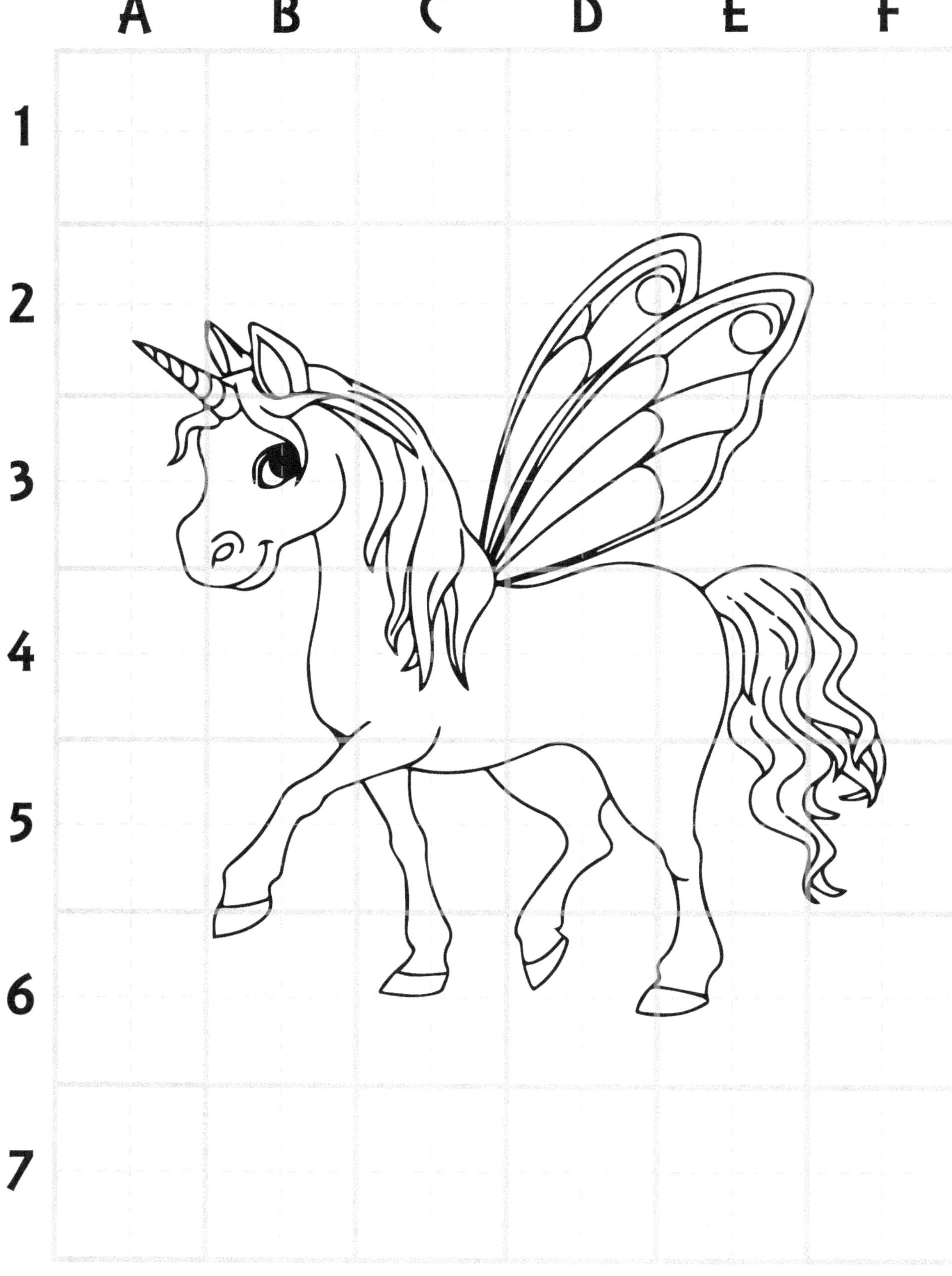

YOUR TURN!

	A	B	C	D	E	F
1						
2						
3						
4						
5						
6						
7						

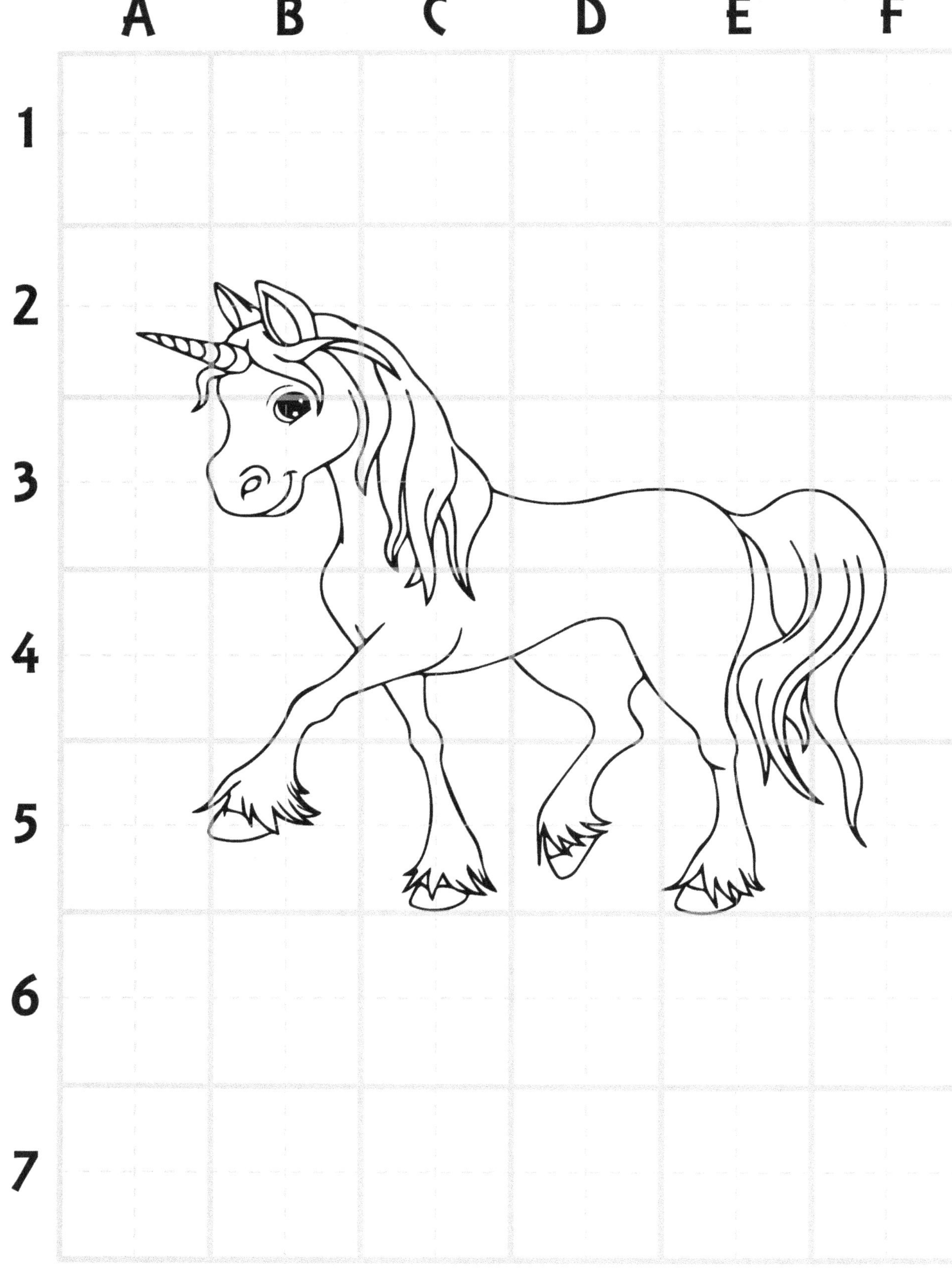

A B C D E F
1
2
3
4
5
6
7

YOUR TURN!

	A	B	C	D	E	F
1						
2						
3						
4						
5						
6						
7						

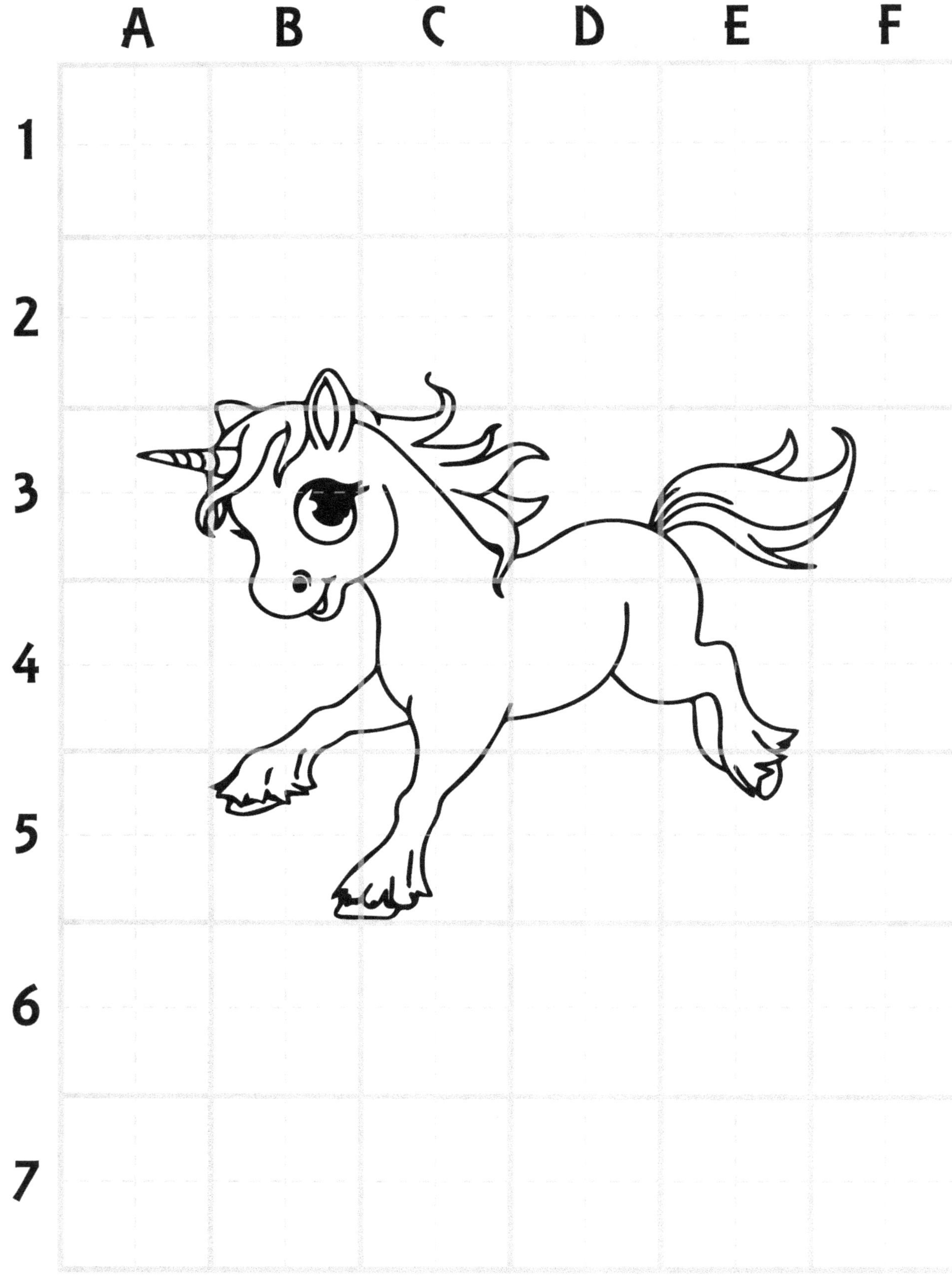

A   B   C   D   E   F
1
2
3
4
5
6
7

YOUR TURN!

	A	B	C	D	E	F
1						
2						
3						
4						
5						
6						
7						

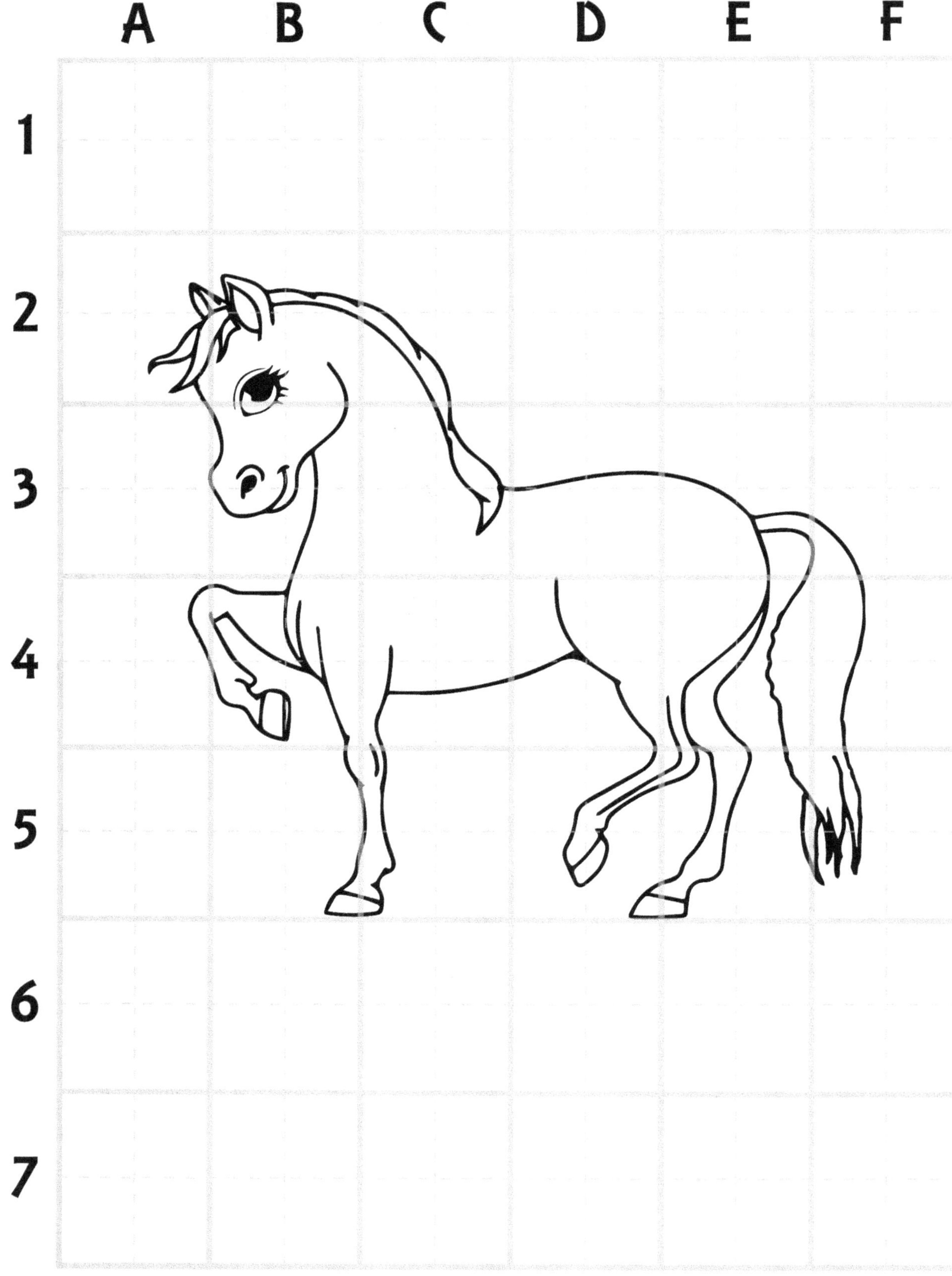

A B C D E F
1
2
3
4
5
6
7

YOUR TURN!

	A	B	C	D	E	F
1						
2						
3						
4						
5						
6						
7						

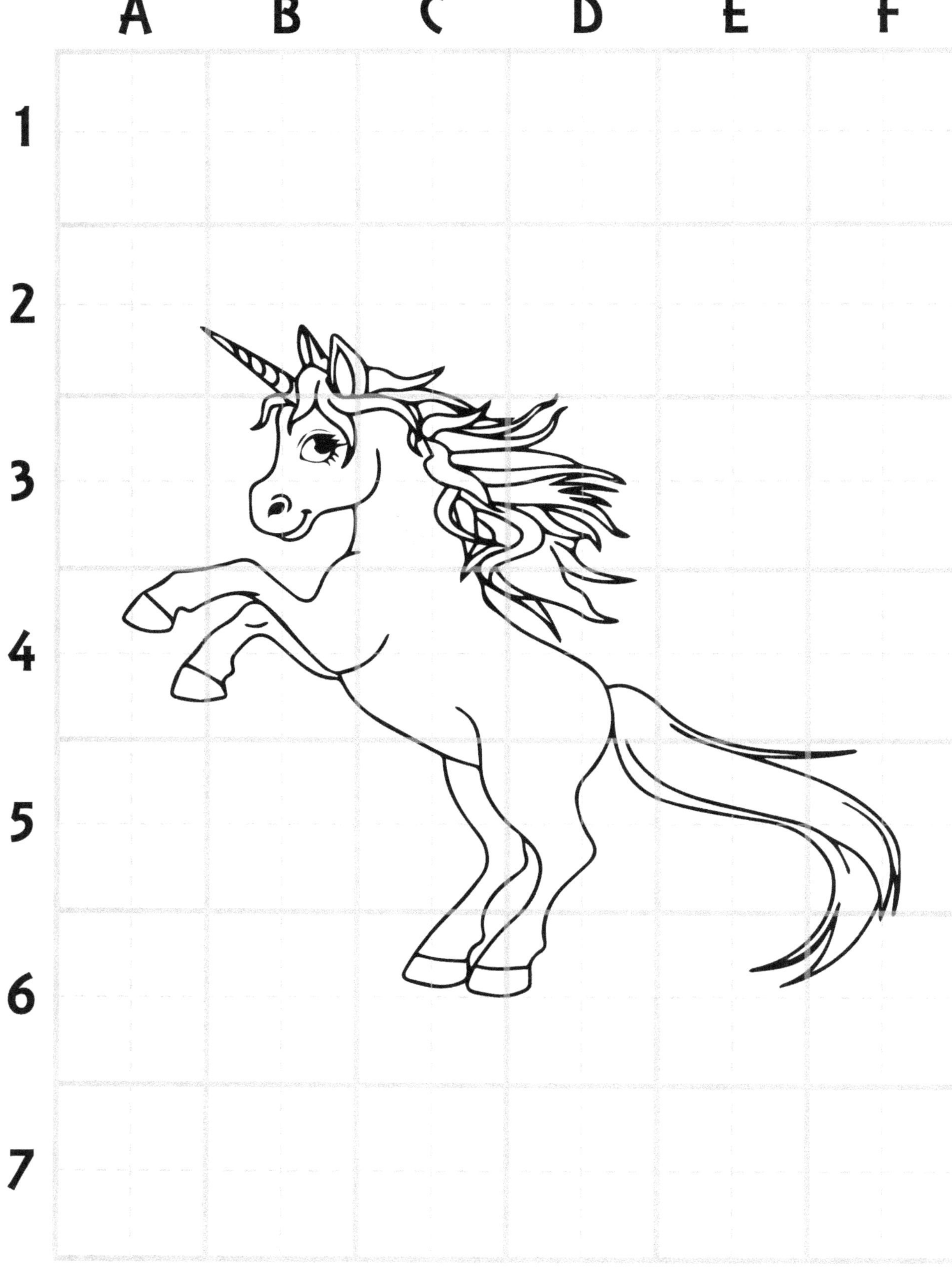

A B C D E F
1
2
3
4
5
6
7

YOUR TURN!

	A	B	C	D	E	F
1						
2						
3						
4						
5						
6						
7						

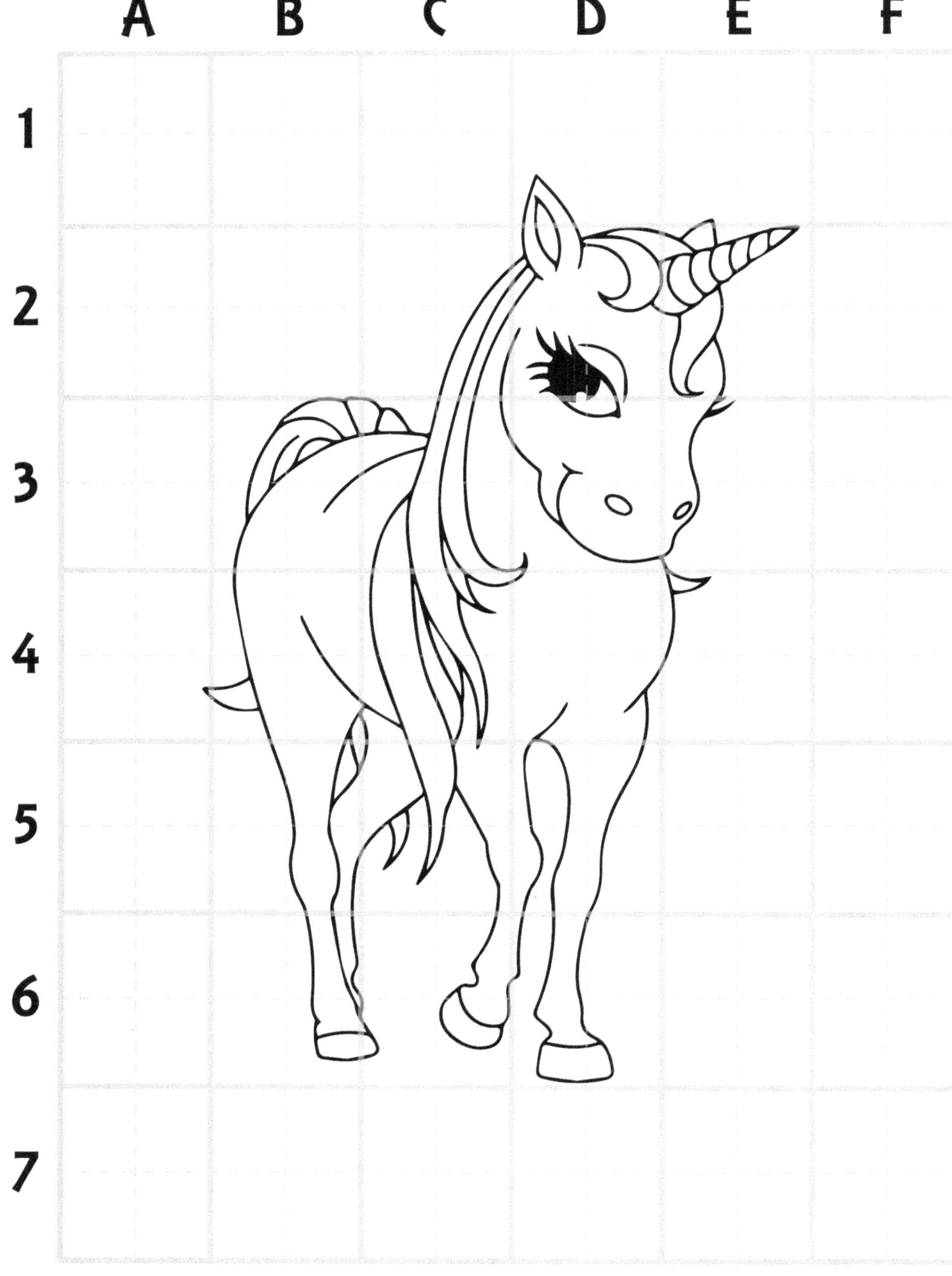

A   B   C   D   E   F
1
2
3
4
5
6
7

YOUR TURN!

	A	B	C	D	E	F
1						
2						
3						
4						
5						
6						
7						

A   B   C   D   E   F
1
2
3
4
5
6
7

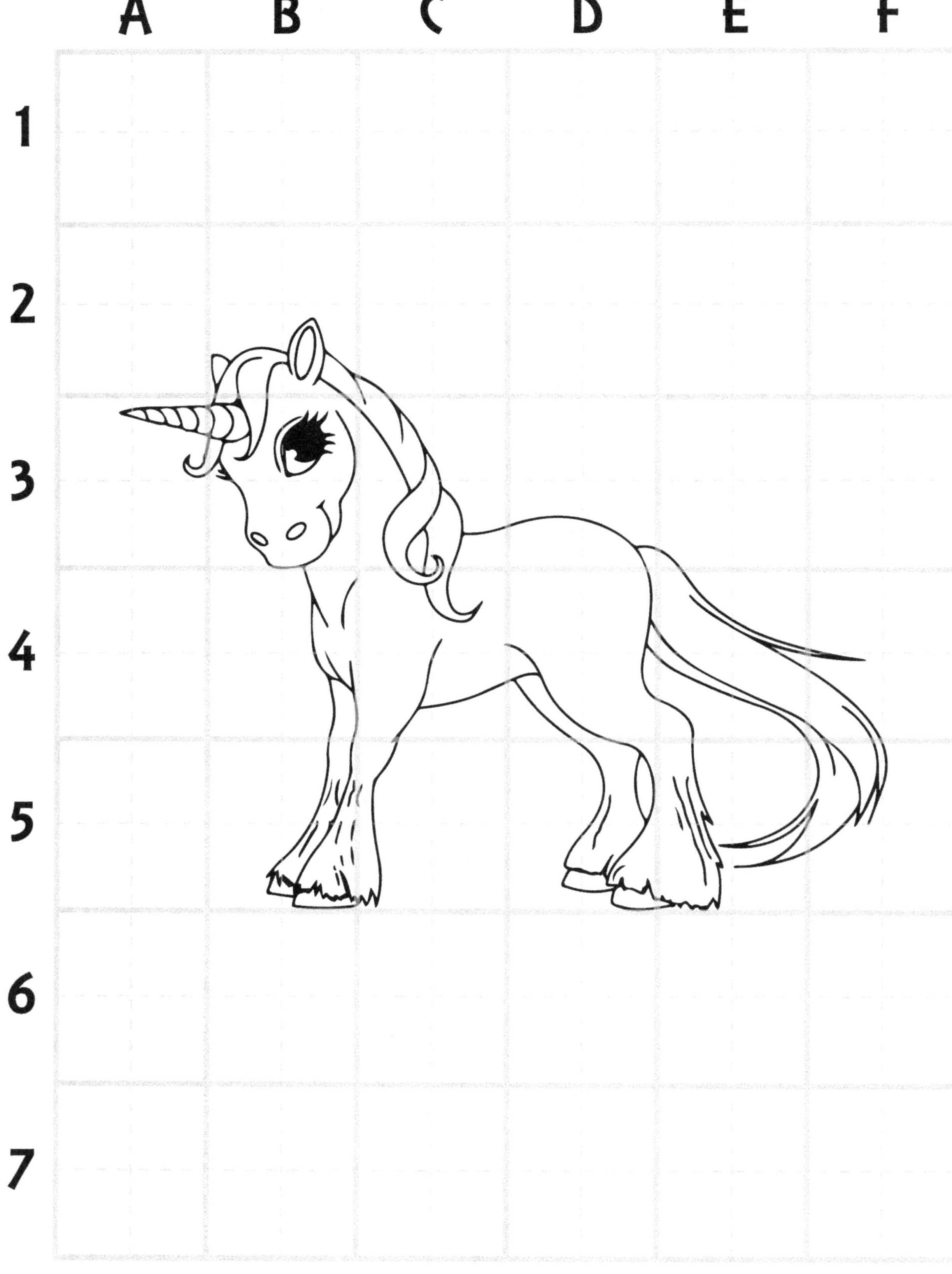

YOUR TURN!

	A	B	C	D	E	F
1						
2						
3						
4						
5						
6						
7						

A B C D E F
1
2
3
4
5
6
7

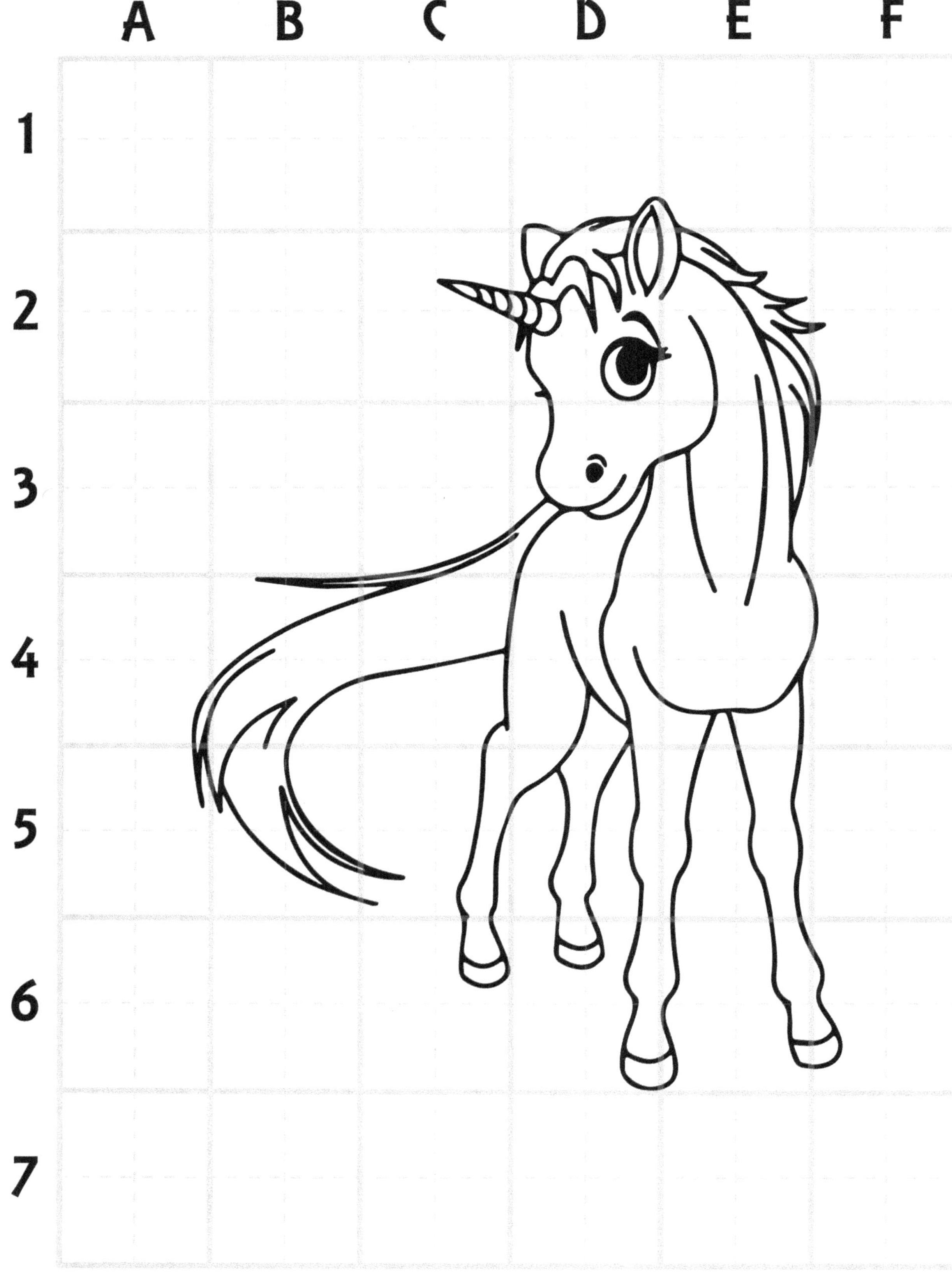

YOUR TURN!

	A	B	C	D	E	F
1						
2						
3						
4						
5						
6						
7						

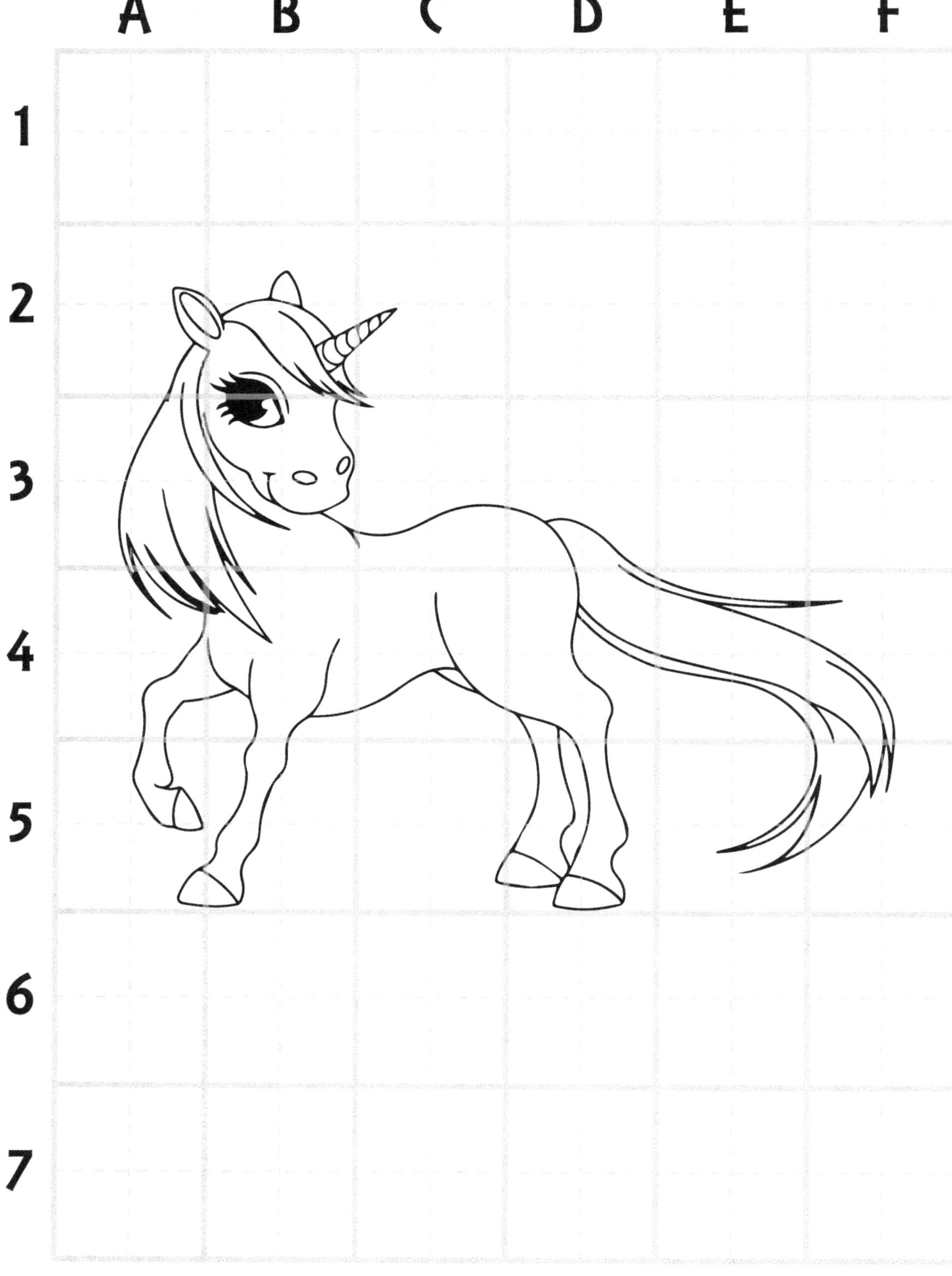

YOUR TURN!

	A	B	C	D	E	F
1						
2						
3						
4						
5						
6						
7						

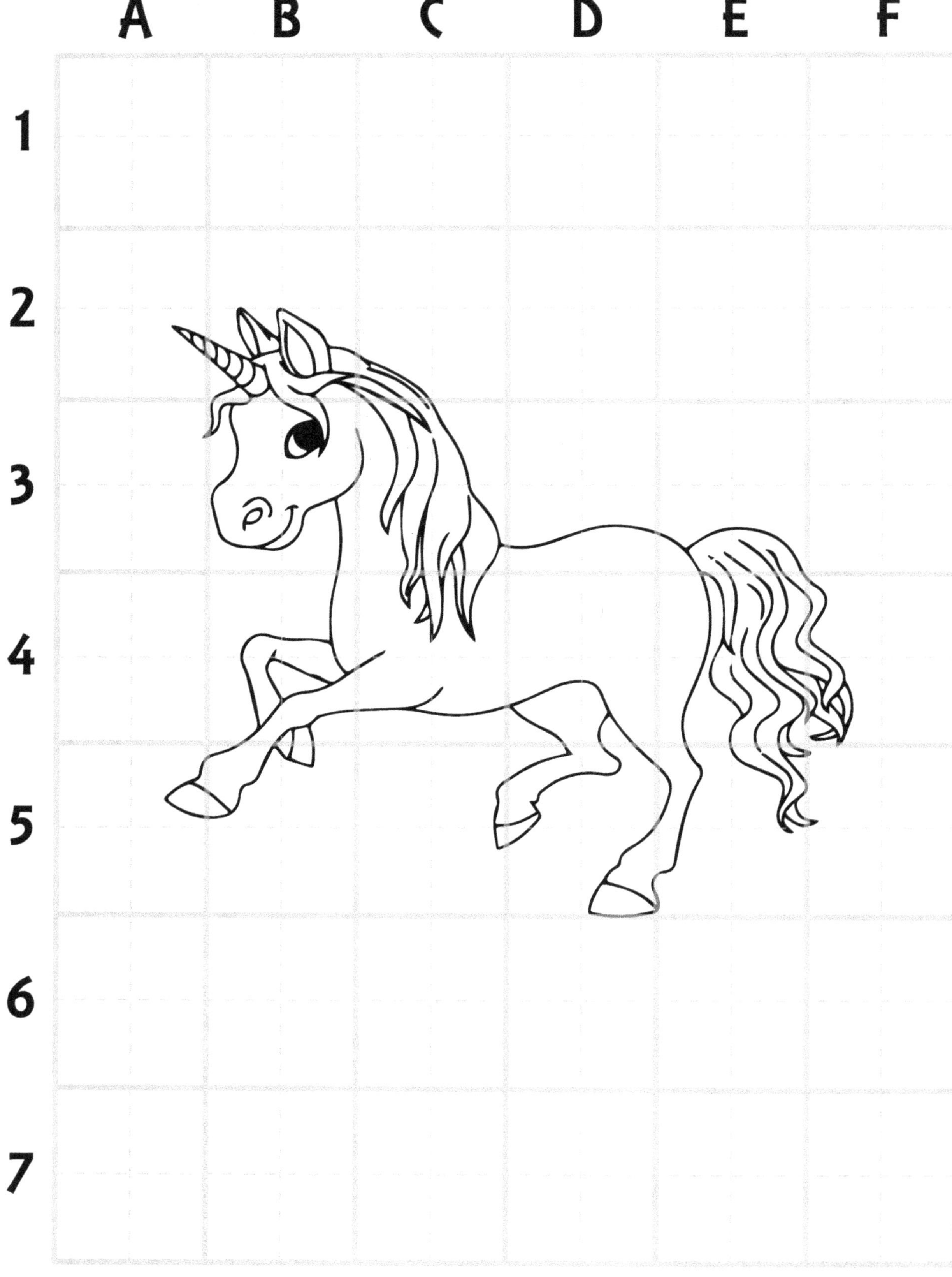

YOUR TURN!

	A	B	C	D	E	F
1						
2						
3						
4						
5						
6						
7						

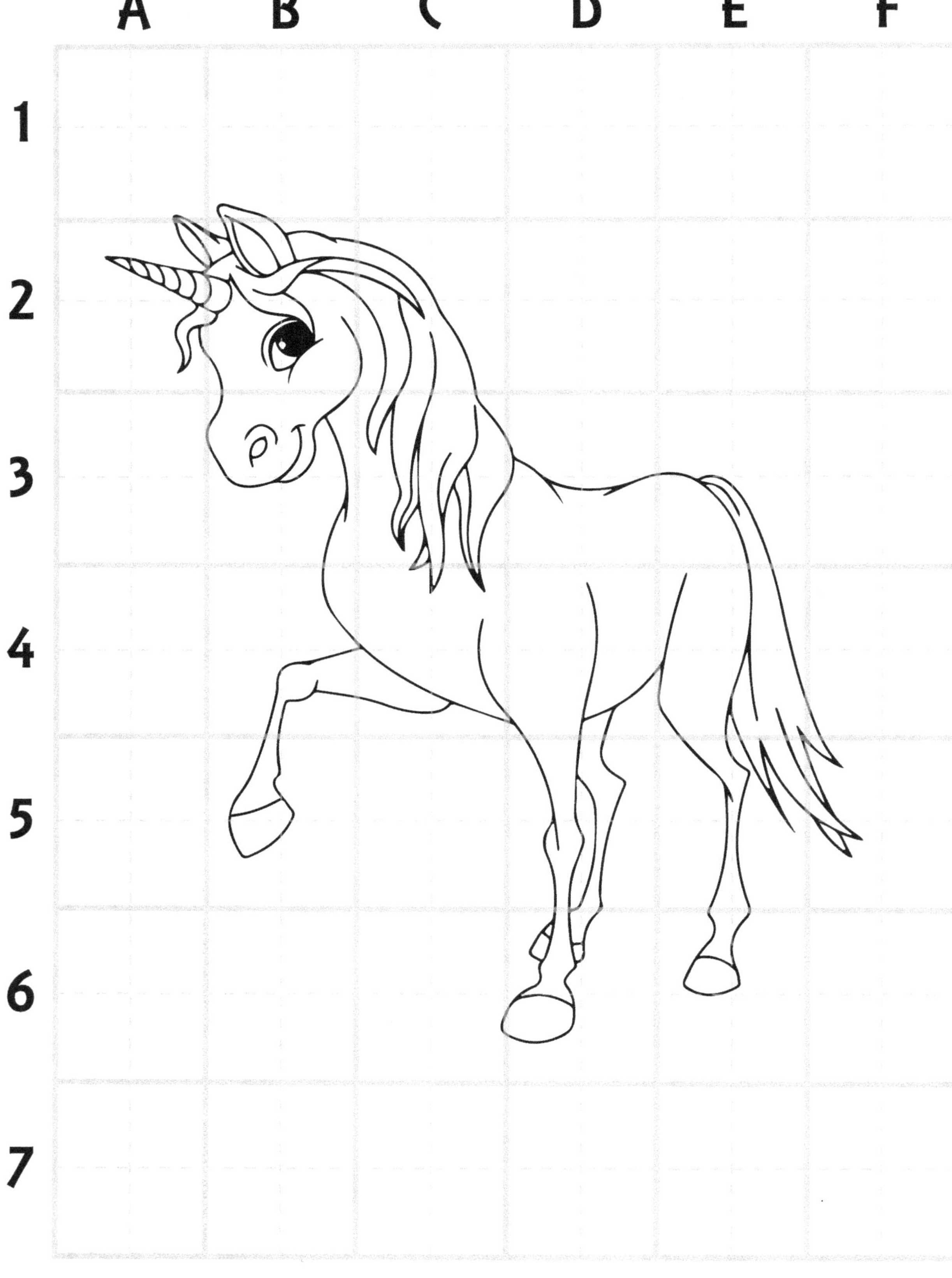

A B C D E F
1
2
3
4
5
6
7

YOUR TURN!

	A	B	C	D	E	F
1						
2						
3						
4						
5						
6						
7						

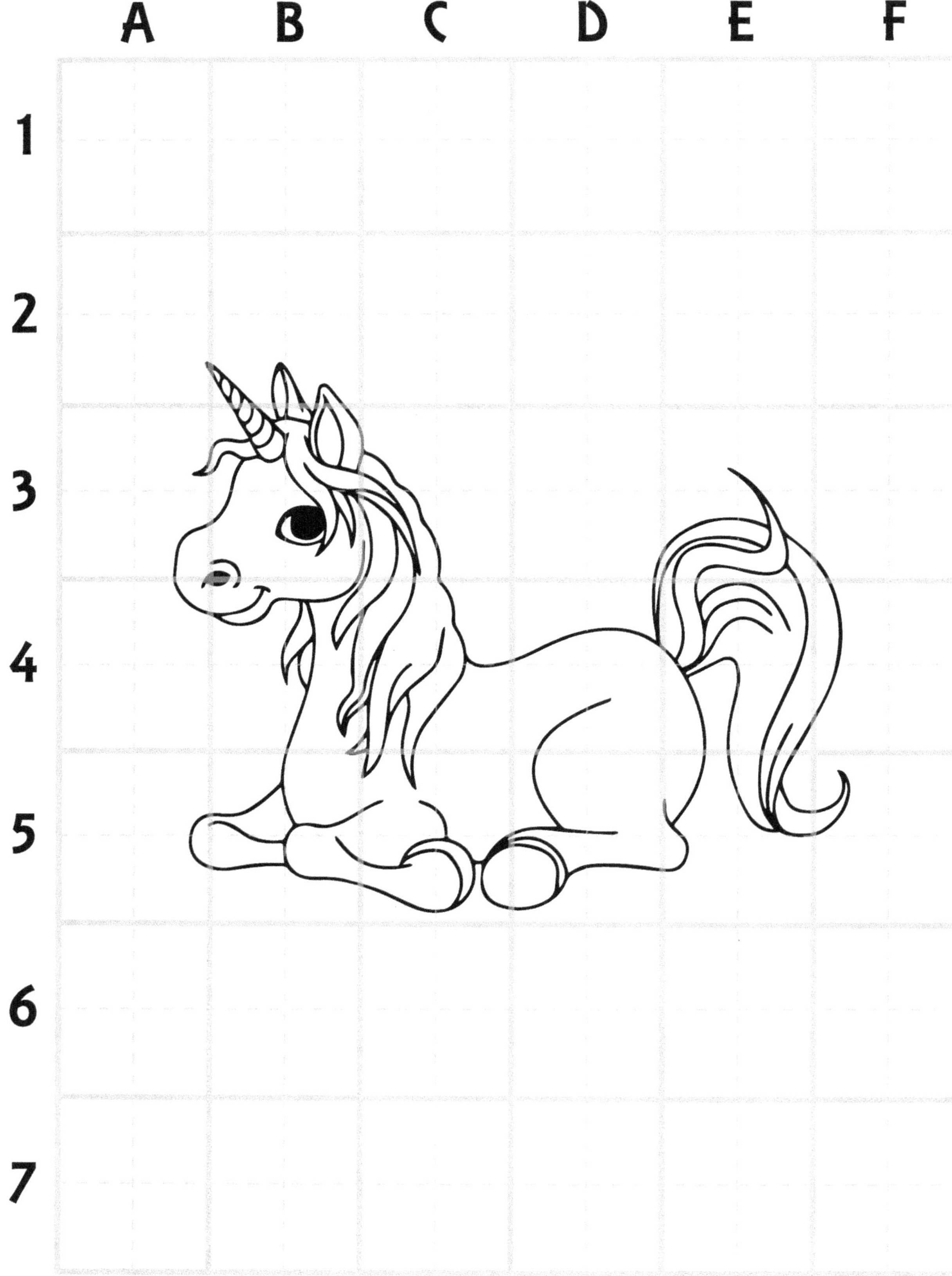

YOUR TURN!

	A	B	C	D	E	F
1						
2						
3						
4						
5						
6						
7						

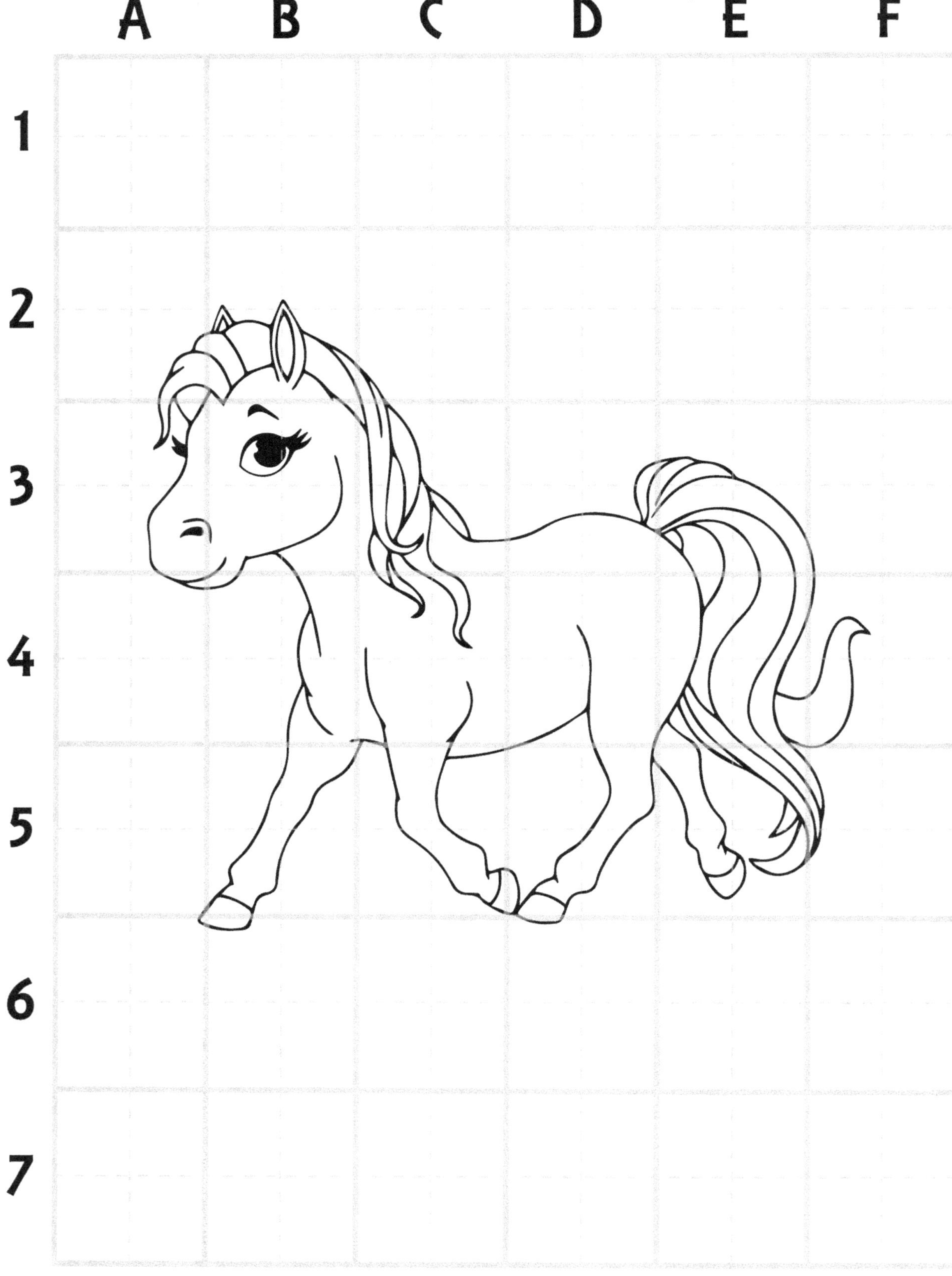

YOUR TURN!

	A	B	C	D	E	F
1						
2						
3						
4						
5						
6						
7						

A B C D E F
1
2
3
4
5
6
7

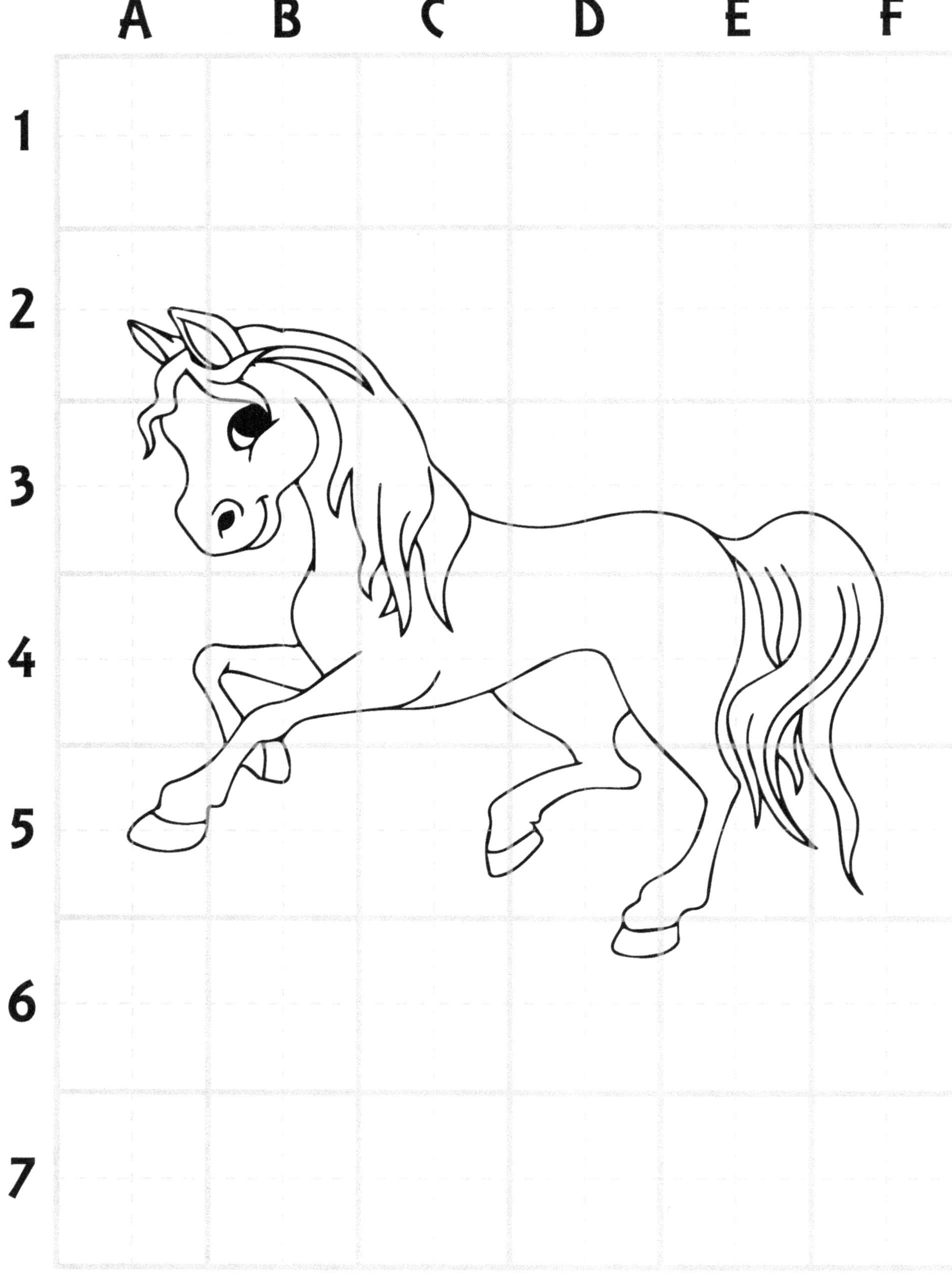

YOUR TURN!

	A	B	C	D	E	F
1						
2						
3						
4						
5						
6						
7						

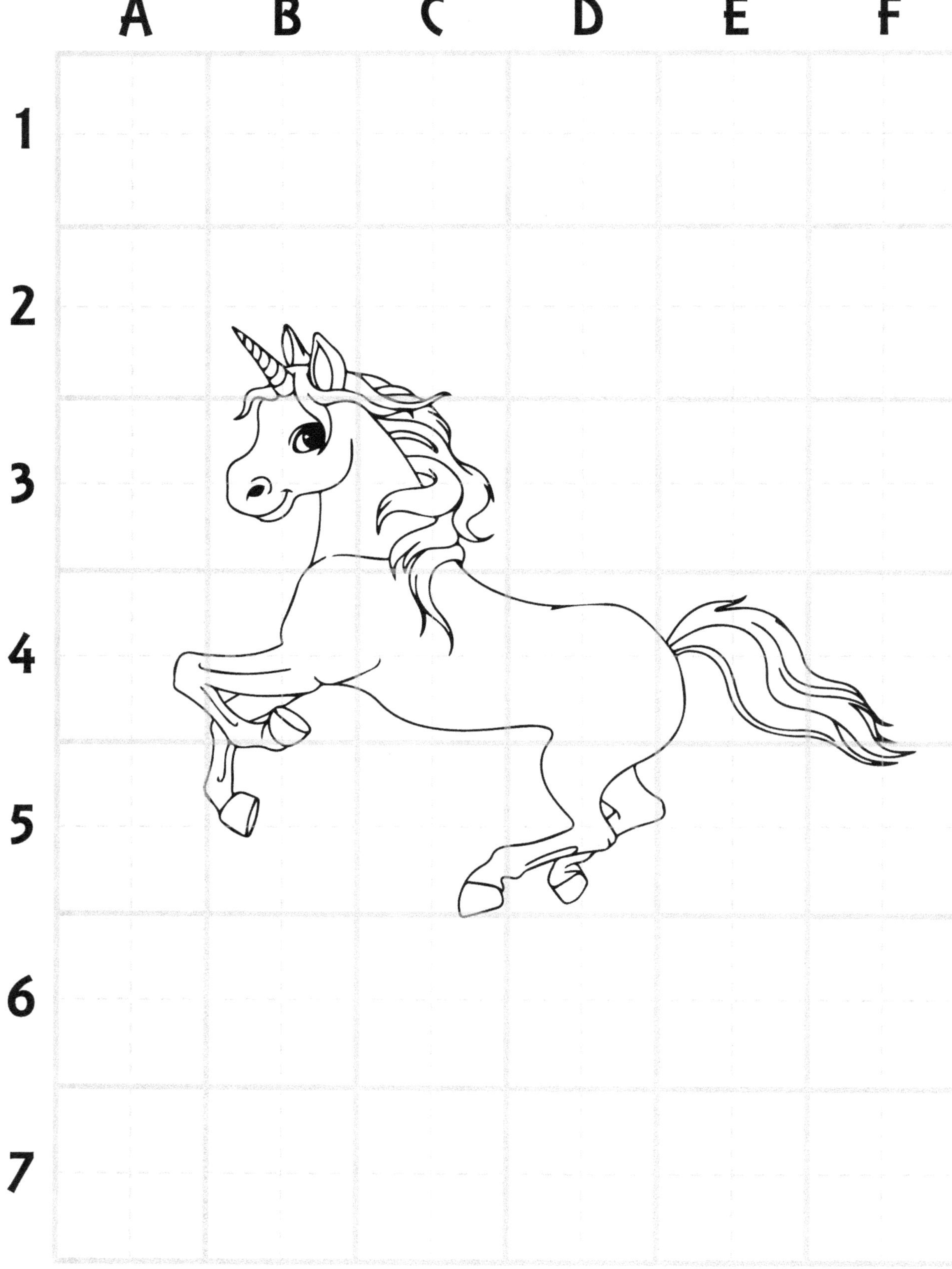

YOUR TURN!

	A	B	C	D	E	F
1						
2						
3						
4						
5						
6						
7						

A B C D E F
1
2
3
4
5
6
7

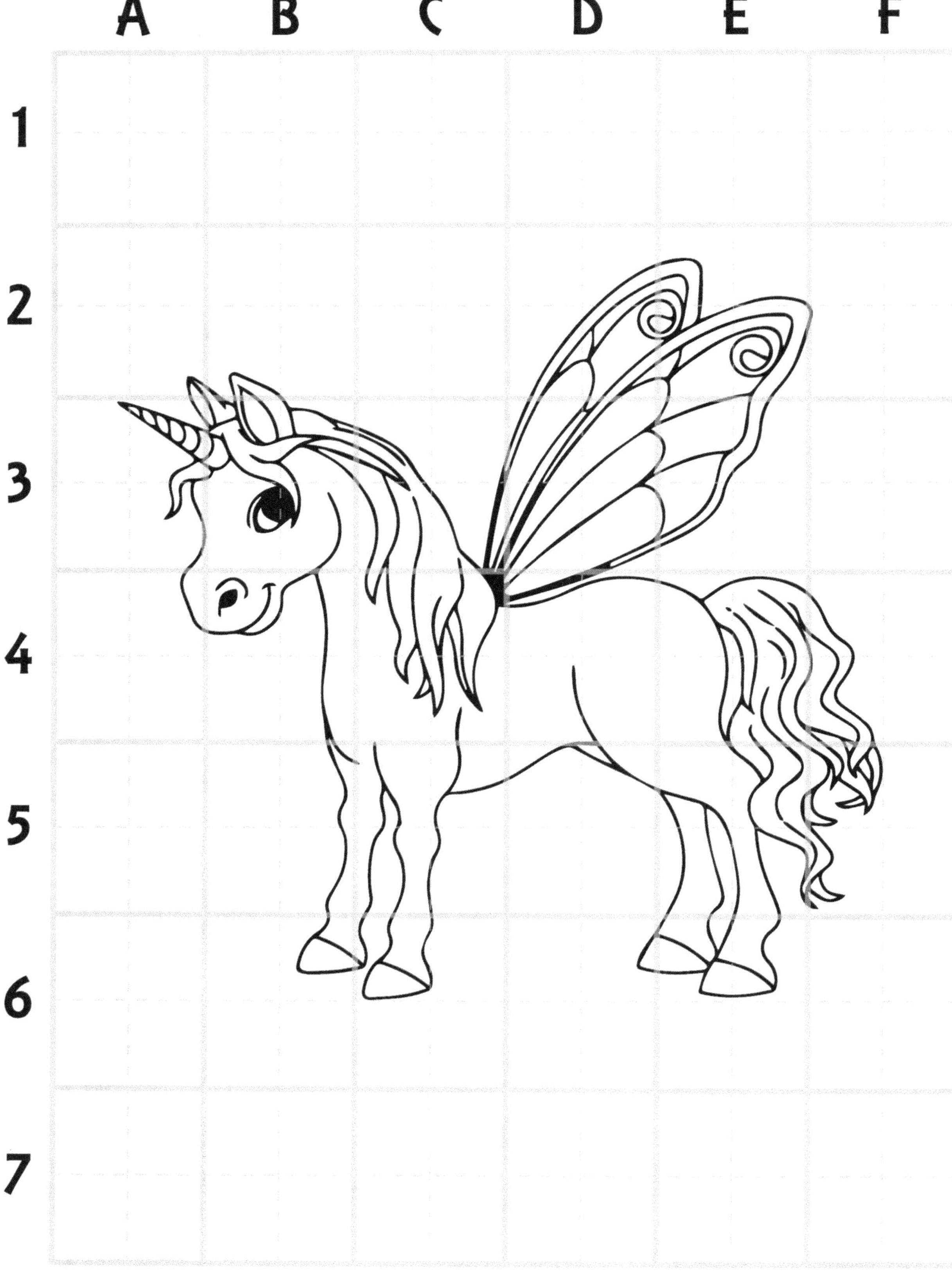

YOUR TURN!

	A	B	C	D	E	F
1						
2						
3						
4						
5						
6						
7						

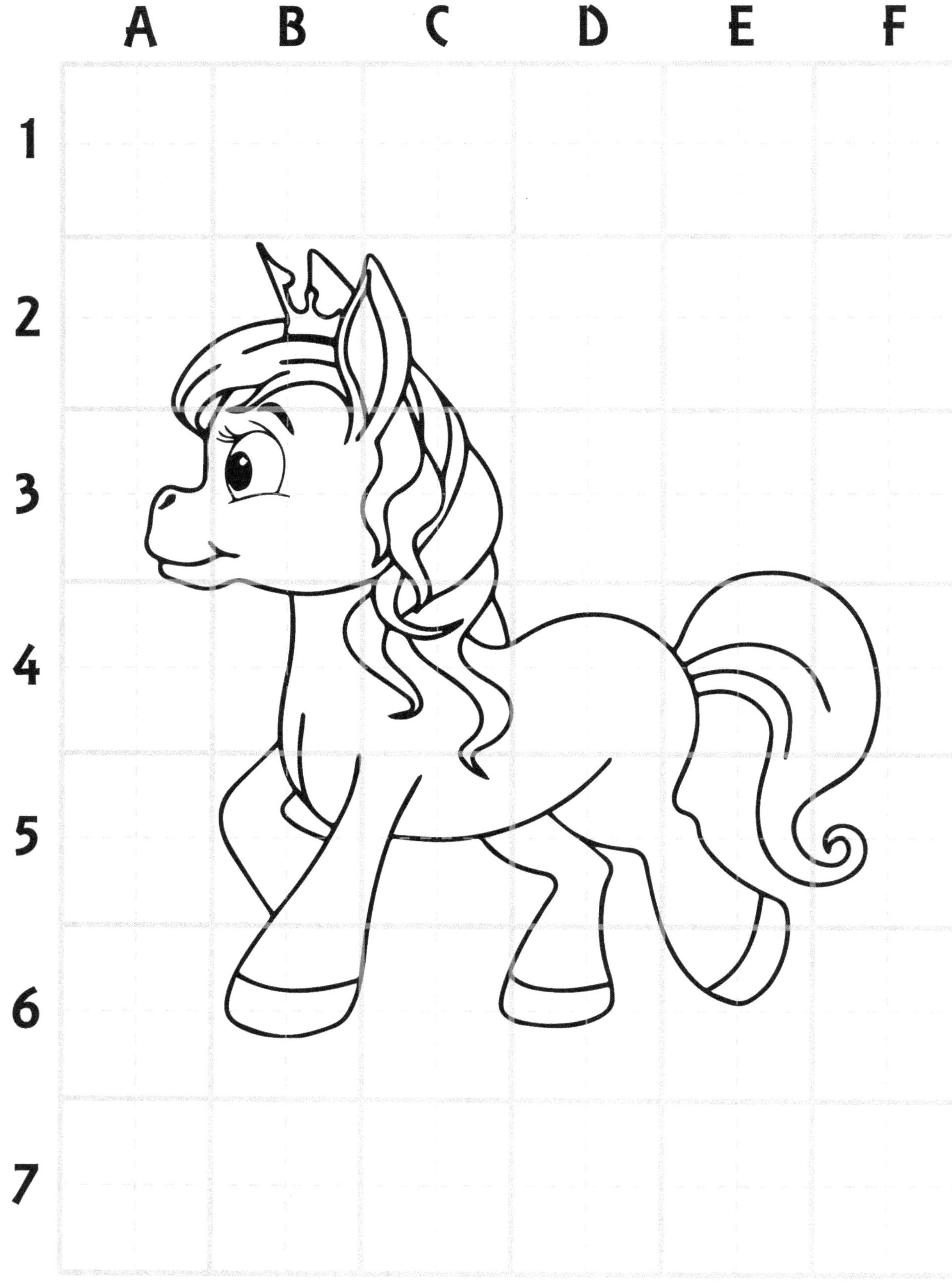

A B C D E F
1
2
3
4
5
6
7

YOUR TURN!

	A	B	C	D	E	F
1						
2						
3						
4						
5						
6						
7						

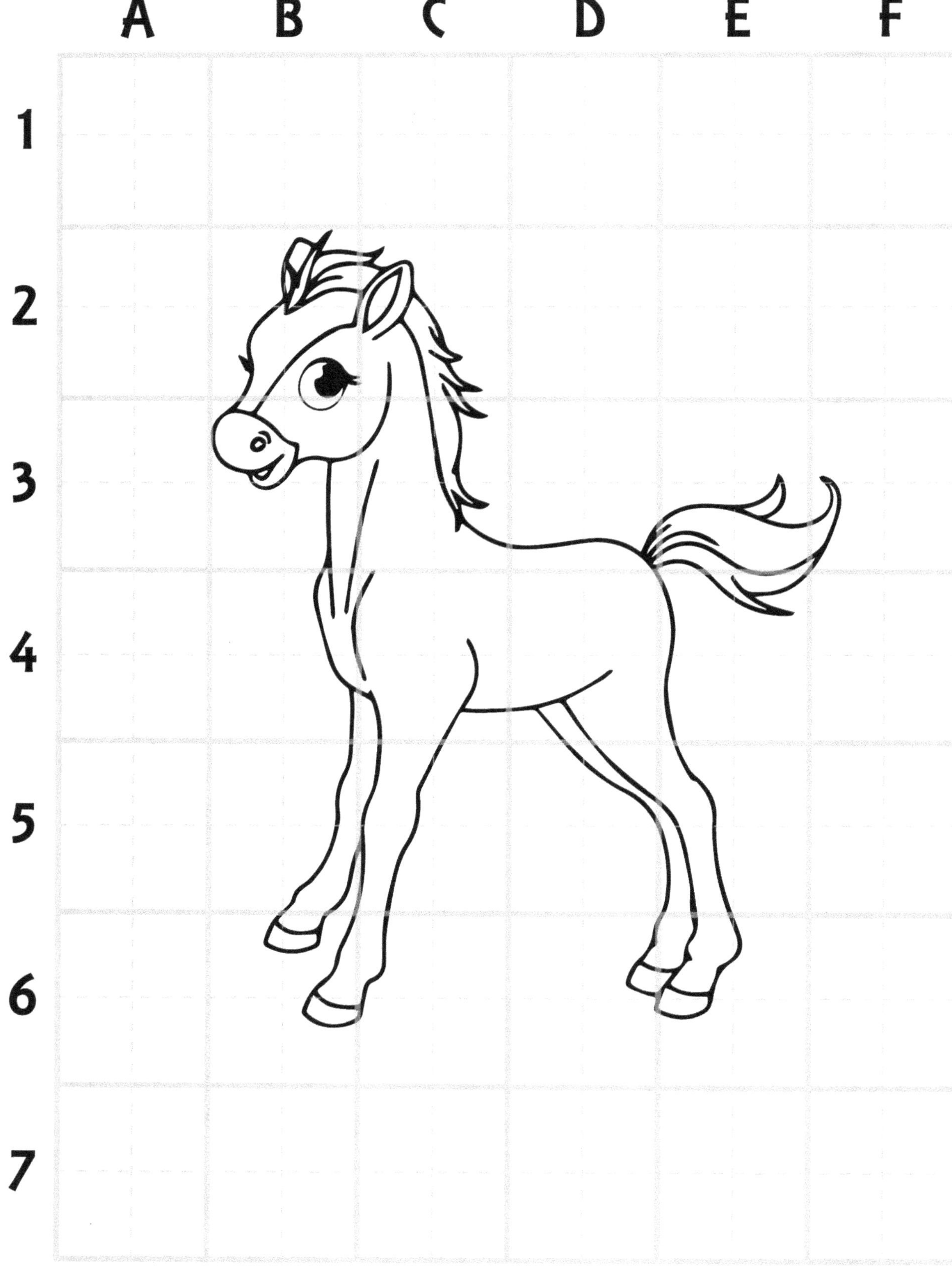
A B C D E F
1
2
3
4
5
6
7

YOUR TURN!

	A	B	C	D	E	F
1						
2						
3						
4						
5						
6						
7						

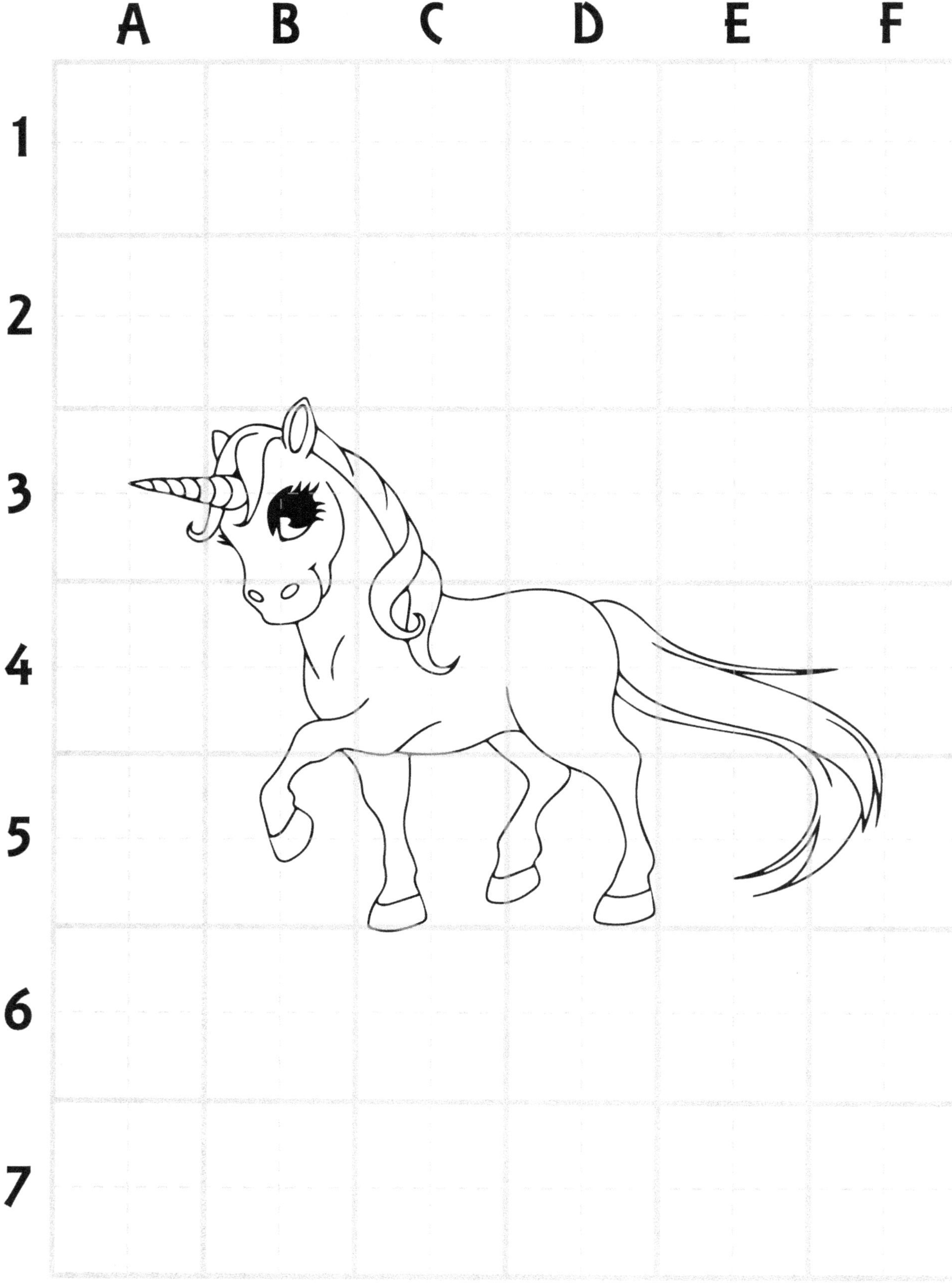

YOUR TURN!

	A	B	C	D	E	F
1						
2						
3						
4						
5						
6						
7						

YOUR TURN!

	A	B	C	D	E	F
1						
2						
3						
4						
5						
6						
7						

YOUR TURN!

	A	B	C	D	E	F
1						
2						
3						
4						
5						
6						
7						

YOUR TURN!

	A	B	C	D	E	F
1						
2						
3						
4						
5						
6						
7						

YOUR TURN!

	A	B	C	D	E	F
1						
2						
3						
4						
5						
6						
7						

YOUR TURN!

	A	B	C	D	E	F
1						
2						
3						
4						
5						
6						
7						

YOUR TURN!

	A	B	C	D	E	F
1						
2						
3						
4						
5						
6						
7						

YOUR TURN!

	A	B	C	D	E	F
1						
2						
3						
4						
5						
6						
7						

YOUR TURN!

	A	B	C	D	E	F
1						
2						
3						
4						
5						
6						
7						

YOUR TURN!

	A	B	C	D	E	F
1						
2						
3						
4						
5						
6						
7						

YOUR TURN!

	A	B	C	D	E	F
1						
2						
3						
4						
5						
6						
7						

YOUR TURN!

	A	B	C	D	E	F
1						
2						
3						
4						
5						
6						
7						

YOUR TURN!

	A	B	C	D	E	F
1						
2						
3						
4						
5						
6						
7						

YOUR TURN!

	A	B	C	D	E	F
1						
2						
3						
4						
5						
6						
7						

YOUR TURN!

	A	B	C	D	E	F
1						
2						
3						
4						
5						
6						
7						

YOUR TURN!

	A	B	C	D	E	F
1						
2						
3						
4						
5						
6						
7						

YOUR TURN!

	A	B	C	D	E	F
1						
2						
3						
4						
5						
6						
7						

YOUR TURN!

<table>
<tr><td></td><td>A</td><td>B</td><td>C</td><td>D</td><td>E</td><td>F</td></tr>
<tr><td>1</td><td></td><td></td><td></td><td></td><td></td><td></td></tr>
<tr><td>2</td><td></td><td></td><td></td><td></td><td></td><td></td></tr>
<tr><td>3</td><td></td><td></td><td></td><td></td><td></td><td></td></tr>
<tr><td>4</td><td></td><td></td><td></td><td></td><td></td><td></td></tr>
<tr><td>5</td><td></td><td></td><td></td><td></td><td></td><td></td></tr>
<tr><td>6</td><td></td><td></td><td></td><td></td><td></td><td></td></tr>
<tr><td>7</td><td></td><td></td><td></td><td></td><td></td><td></td></tr>
</table>

YOUR TURN!

	A	B	C	D	E	F
1						
2						
3						
4						
5						
6						
7						

YOUR TURN!

	A	B	C	D	E	F
1						
2						
3						
4						
5						
6						
7						

YOUR TURN!

	A	B	C	D	E	F
1						
2						
3						
4						
5						
6						
7						

YOUR TURN!

	A	B	C	D	E	F
1						
2						
3						
4						
5						
6						
7						

YOUR TURN!

	A	B	C	D	E	F
1						
2						
3						
4						
5						
6						
7						

YOUR TURN!

	A	B	C	D	E	F
1						
2						
3						
4						
5						
6						
7						

YOUR TURN!

	A	B	C	D	E	F
1						
2						
3						
4						
5						
6						
7						

YOUR TURN!

	A	B	C	D	E	F
1						
2						
3						
4						
5						
6						
7						

YOUR TURN!

	A	B	C	D	E	F
1						
2						
3						
4						
5						
6						
7						

YOUR TURN!

	A	B	C	D	E	F
1						
2						
3						
4						
5						
6						
7						

YOUR TURN!

	A	B	C	D	E	F
1						
2						
3						
4						
5						
6						
7						

YOUR TURN!

	A	B	C	D	E	F
1						
2						
3						
4						
5						
6						
7						

YOUR TURN!

	A	B	C	D	E	F
1						
2						
3						
4						
5						
6						
7						

YOUR TURN!

	A	B	C	D	E	F
1						
2						
3						
4						
5						
6						
7						

YOUR TURN!

	A	B	C	D	E	F
1						
2						
3						
4						
5						
6						
7						

YOUR TURN!

	A	B	C	D	E	F
1						
2						
3						
4						
5						
6						
7						

YOUR TURN!

	A	B	C	D	E	F
1						
2						
3						
4						
5						
6						
7						

YOUR TURN!

	A	B	C	D	E	F
1						
2						
3						
4						
5						
6						
7						

YOUR TURN!

	A	B	C	D	E	F
1						
2						
3						
4						
5						
6						
7						

YOUR TURN!

	A	B	C	D	E	F
1						
2						
3						
4						
5						
6						
7						

YOUR TURN!

	A	B	C	D	E	F
1						
2						
3						
4						
5						
6						
7						

YOUR TURN!

	A	B	C	D	E	F
1						
2						
3						
4						
5						
6						
7						

YOUR TURN!

	A	B	C	D	E	F
1						
2						
3						
4						
5						
6						
7						

YOUR TURN!

	A	B	C	D	E	F
1						
2						
3						
4						
5						
6						
7						

YOUR TURN!

	A	B	C	D	E	F
1						
2						
3						
4						
5						
6						
7						

YOUR TURN!

	A	B	C	D	E	F
1						
2						
3						
4						
5						
6						
7						

YOUR TURN!

	A	B	C	D	E	F
1						
2						
3						
4						
5						
6						
7						

YOUR TURN!

	A	B	C	D	E	F
1						
2						
3						
4						
5						
6						
7						

YOUR TURN!

	A	B	C	D	E	F
1						
2						
3						
4						
5						
6						
7						

YOUR TURN!

	A	B	C	D	E	F
1						
2						
3						
4						
5						
6						
7						

YOUR TURN!

	A	B	C	D	E	F
1						
2						
3						
4						
5						
6						
7						

YOUR TURN!

	A	B	C	D	E	F
1						
2						
3						
4						
5						
6						
7						

YOUR TURN!

	A	B	C	D	E	F
1						
2						
3						
4						
5						
6						
7						

YOUR TURN!

	A	B	C	D	E	F
1						
2						
3						
4						
5						
6						
7						

YOUR TURN!

	A	B	C	D	E	F
1						
2						
3						
4						
5						
6						
7						

YOUR TURN!

	A	B	C	D	E	F
1						
2						
3						
4						
5						
6						
7						

YOUR TURN!

	A	B	C	D	E	F
1						
2						
3						
4						
5						
6						
7						

YOUR TURN!

	A	B	C	D	E	F
1						
2						
3						
4						
5						
6						
7						

YOUR TURN!

	A	B	C	D	E	F
1						
2						
3						
4						
5						
6						
7						

YOUR TURN!

	A	B	C	D	E	F
1						
2						
3						
4						
5						
6						
7